THE ART OF
CREATIVE MATTING

THE ART OF
CREATIVE MATTING

TECHNIQUES, DESIGN APPLICATIONS, AND PRICING FOR PROFITABILITY

Sean Hunt, CPF
Valerie McClure, CPF

✦ ESSELTE LETRASET

Trademarks

Ronsonol® is a registered trademark of Ronson Corp., Woodbridge, NJ.

Scotch™ is a trademark of 3M Corp., St. Paul, MN.

Super-Kote™ is a trademark of Products Distributors, San Antonio, TX.

Tri-Flow™ is a trademark of Richardson-Vicks, Inc., Memphis, TN.

Dexter® is a registered trademark of Russell Harrington Cutlery, Inc., Southbridge, MA.

Alphamat®, Alpharag®, C & H/Bainbridge®, Nielsen®, and Oval-Master® are registered trademarks of Nielsen & Bainbridge, a division of Esselte Pendaflex Corp., Garden City, NY.

Black by Bainbridge™ is a trademark of Nielsen & Bainbridge, a division of Esselte Pendaflex Corp., Garden City, NY.

WD-40® is a registered trademark of WD-40 Co., San Diego, CA.

Teflon® is a registered trademark of E.I. DuPont de Nemours & Co., Inc., Wilmington, DE.

NIELSEN & BAINBRIDGE

Paramus, New Jersey

Printed in the United States of America.
ISBN: 0-9618735-0-7

TITLE: PPFA Code of Ethics

**1st Place Winner
1983 PPFA—New York
New and Creative Framing Competition**

Preface

Among the many skills that are essential to being a Custom Picture Framer, none is as rewarding as that of mat cutting. Developing the necessary technique to conceive and execute a beautiful mat or combination of mats can be crucial to establishing your reputation as a "creative" framer, for this skill is one of the primary criteria upon which you will be judged by your customers.

This ability and its recognition by your clients can be one of the key factors that separates you from your competition. Displaying and designing "Creative Matting" will bring you more and better framing business than anything else we know of.

Not to be ignored is the concrete fact that there is more profit in matting than in any other area of framing. While we all pay essentially the same for a piece of matboard, the only thing that limits how much we can charge the customer for that same piece of board is what we create with it. Every time you make a cut in the board you can expect compensation. *Remember* you are no longer charging for time and materials, but rather for your "Creativity and Design" ability. These are skills that you can turn into substantial profit and recognition for you and your gallery/frameshop.

While we think that most framers would agree with the importance of being "creative" with their matting, it has previously been very difficult if not impossible to find instruction in how to develop the skills. Our aim in writing this book is to provide framers with a text that will teach them to execute creative cuts and corners, give guidance in where to use those same techniques when designing specific framings, and last, but probably most important, how to charge so that they will receive a profitable return on their new creativity.

It is our hope that you will find the designs and techniques in this book to be stimulating and exciting and that your enthusiasm will transfer to your customers and bring you the satisfaction and rewards they have brought to both of us over the past fifteen years.

Contents

PART 5   CONCLUDING THOUGHTS   159

INTRODUCTION:

How to Use This Book

Our two main objectives in writing this text are, first, to present as many "creative" techniques as possible to the reader and, second, to make the material covered easy to understand. The book is intended to be a working tool; one that the framer can refer to constantly for assistance in designing, as well as executing, "creative" matting.

With that in mind, as you progress through the book, you will find color photographs on the pages near the step-by-step instructions for executing a particular design. These pictures will enable you to see what the finished product of the technique you are working on is going to look like. We also include photographs of some variations on the basic idea in order to give your creative juices a little extra stimulation.

Following this introduction, the book is broken down into five sections. Part 1 contains general information that will help you to get started, including a very important section on cleaning and lubricating the mat cutter. It also discusses proper mat cutting techniques and offers some solutions to possible problems with bad cuts.

Part 2 covers some beginning techniques and concepts that are an *essential* foundation for developing more complicated design skills. This will include an introduction to the "V-Groove" technique, which is the basis for all of the "creative" mat designs discussed in this book. Part 2 continues with an introductory section on pricing that presents all of the factors to be considered when determining charges for a specific type of matboard and design, including a recommended charge for each technique discussed thus far. From that point on, as you learn each new technique, there will be a recommended pricing charge given. Some of you may find these recommended charges too high or too low, but they will at least give you an idea of where to start in establishing your own pricing structure. In order to provide you with an easy and complete reference on pricing, the charges for all of the techniques and designs covered in this volume are summarized in Appendix A.

In Part 3 we begin to cover more advanced techniques of "Creative Matting" and discuss the "Slant Corner" concept, another extremely important and fundamental step. We also continue to give you tips on pricing and designing.

Part 4 discusses the use of a circle/oval mat cutter. We will begin by explaining how to cut a single oval or circular mat, then proceed to double ovals and circles, adding a "V-Groove" for design, and finally designs that involve using both a straight line cutter and a circle/oval machine. Along the way there are many tips on designing with these techniques and, as always, our recommended pricing.

Part 5 contains photographs of some finished framing designs that we consider to be among the best we've done. We include them in the hope that they will stimulate your creativity as you explore the material covered in this text.

The material is presented in sequence, with each technique building on the previous one. As such, the book has been designed for you to use as a workbook. By absorbing the ideas in each chapter, practicing the cuts, and then creating working samples, you will find it very easy to progress from the basic to the more advanced and exotic concepts.

However, for those readers who are more advanced, please feel free to skip around to those sections that contain new and unfamiliar material. The method for executing each technique will be covered in a step-by-step fashion, and you should have no difficulty creating any of the designs if you follow our instructions. In those cases where we anticipate that there may be some confusion for you, we have included diagrams to indicate exactly where to mark and cut your mat. Our primary goal in writing this book has been to make it as useful and self-explanatory as possible.

As you proceed through this book, please keep in mind that our thoughts on design are only suggestions for you to use in developing your own matting tastes. All the ideas and designs presented are used continually in my framing and gallery business, and we're certain of their ability to please your customers and help merchandise your art inventory. Still, there is never just a single "creative" way to mat something, so be sure to do plenty of experimenting on your own. You will be amazed at all the great looking mats you can develop.

Whatever method you choose for exploring our material, we hope it will inspire and stimulate your creativity, make your everyday job as a professional framer a little bit simpler, and bring you increased personal satisfaction and profits. **GOOD LUCK!**

1

GENERAL INFORMATION ABOUT MAT CUTTING

Getting Started: What Do You Need?

We would like to begin by stating that all of the cuts and corner designs shown in this book were achieved with a straight line mat cutter, an oval/circle mat cutter, or a combination of the two. None of the work shown or discussed was done by a so-called "Freehand Cutting" method. Don't misunderstand, there is some outstanding work being done by a number of very "creative" framers who cut some or all of their mats freehanded. It is simply a skill that we don't have. One of the beauties of our system is that it is all accomplished on a mat cutting machine that is readily available to every framer. You will not need special skills to achieve any of the beautiful and highly creative mats we teach in this book.

As you are probably aware, there are a number of these straight line mat cutters available in the industry. While it is not intended as a recommendation to buy or any guarantee of success with the cuts and designs portrayed in this text, we will tell you that all of the examples pictured (as well as all of our day-to-day framing work) have been executed with a C & H/Bainbridge mat cutter (see page 6).

We should also mention that all of the designs and techniques that are shown and discussed can be executed with any type or brand of matboard you wish to use.

In addition to a mat cutter, a mat marking guide is the only other item we feel is essential for accurate and professional execution of the mats discussed in this book. Since a guide is included with most new mat cutters, this statement may seem to be unnecessary. However, after almost ten years of teaching seminars and workshops throughout this country and in Canada, we have found that there are a suprisingly large number of framers who have a mat marking guide and don't use it. Once

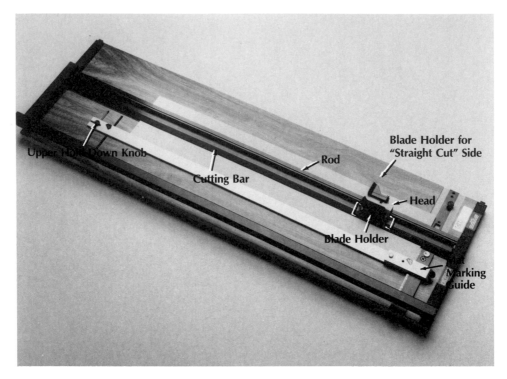

C & H/Bainbridge Mat Cutter—Model 4060B

again, there is nothing wrong with marking your mats by hand. *However, it can never be as fast or, most importantly, as accurate as doing it with a guide.* As we progress through this book and you actually begin to execute what you are learning, you will quickly see that one of the key elements to obtaining professional results is precision. *So **use your mat marking guide**.*

You will not need the adjustable stops or any other attachments for the mat cutter in order to execute the material in this volume. The stops are designed to facilitate high volume mat cutting, and while certain of the mats can be accomplished using the stops, most of them cannot. As many of you have discovered, the stops require constant adjustment in order to consistently eliminate overcuts. Because of this, it is essential to polish your cutting technique and learn to judge the proper amount of overcut and undercut by eye. Since we will be marking all of our mats, we recommend using a no. 4 extra hard pencil (never a ball point pen) and keeping it *sharp*.

For those mats that will require pieces being taped together (these would include "V-Groove" mats and Inlay mats), we recommend *only* 3M Scotch® Brand 810 Magic Transparent Tape. For taping two or more mats together, we use 3M Scotch Brand 924 or 969 Adhesive Transfer

Tape. This tape is widely used in the framing industry for this as well as a number of other applications and is generally referred to as ATG. The 969 ATG is quite a bit stronger and stickier than the 924.

Finally, we cannot say enough about the need for you to spend some time practicing the things that are presented in this book. While we will be showing you in a step-by-step fashion how to achieve every cut we know, we cannot teach you how to cut a perfect mat. Only time, practice, and cutting a lot of mats will accomplish that. We know how busy you all are and that there never seems to be enough time to get all the customer work done, much less practice cutting mats. And yet, you must. Try to put in some time either before you open or after you close each day: just a half hour will bring substantial improvement very quickly. The important thing is to practice every day until it becomes second nature. It's like riding a bike: once learned you won't forget.

Cleaning and Lubricating the Cutter

A mat cutter, like all precision equipment, has to be properly maintained. The key step to this maintenance is regular and proper cleaning and lubrication, and there is an excellent method to learn before going any further in this text. We cannot overemphasize how important this section is, for not only will proper cleaning and lubrication insure a long life for your mat cutter, but a smooth running cutter will make it much easier for you to execute the "Creative Techniques" presented throughout this book.

To begin with, we recommend that your mat cutter be cleaned and lubricated every time that you use it. This regular schedule will insure that the cutter always works easily and smoothly. It also minimizes the wear on the bar, rod, and block.

The items you will need for our cleaning/lubrication procedure are

- A can of lighter fluid.

- A box of cotton swabs.

- Facial tissue or toilet tissue.

- A can of Super-Kote™ Lubricant.

For those readers who are not familiar with Super-Kote, it is a wax based lubricant which contains no oil at all, and is in our opinion the best product available for use on the mat cutter. We have found some framers who prefer to use a Teflon® lubricant called Tri-Flow®, and we do consider it an acceptable substitute. However, *we do not recommend the use of silicone, WD-40®, or any other lubricant that contains oil.* Not only does oil tend to attract and coagulate dirt, it also "hangs in the air" in your shop and can transfer to artwork that you are in the process of framing.

There are two additional advantages of Super-Kote that are worth pointing out. First, it has a tendency not to attract dirt which can gum up the cutter. Second, if your cutter should develop a stickiness during the working day, Super-Kote can be lightly sprayed on the trouble area (or the full length of the cutting bar if necessary), wiped off, and you will be immediately able to resume cutting mats. This is quite different from Silicone or other oil-type lubricants, for once the cutter begins to gum up, the only cure is to strip the bar and rod down with a solvent and then reapply the lubricant. If you have been using another type of lubricant, we would strongly suggest that you at least give Super-Kote a try. It is currently available from most major framing supply companies.

Once you have all the necessary materials, follow the recommended procedure below for first cleaning your mat cutter and then applying the lubricant of your choice.

1. Remove the blade from the cutting head on your mat cutter.

2. Put the nozzle of the lighter fluid can just in front of where the cutting head fits over the rod on the cutting bar. Apply lighter fluid liberally while moving the cutting head up and down the length of the rod. This will flush out any buildup of dirt that has accumulated inside the cutting head. (See photo on page 10.)

3. Place the head of a cotton swab where the rod joins the cutting bar and run it up and down the full length of the bar. Do this on both sides of the rod. If this is your first time using this cleaning method, you'll be quite surprised at the amount of gunk you'll find on the cotton swab.

4. Wipe the rod and cutting bar down thoroughly until all traces of lighter fluid are gone. You should also lift the cutting bar up and dry off the underside. Finally, be sure to wipe off any lighter fluid that might have accumulated on the surface of the mat cutter base.

5. Spray Super-Kote *lightly* along the length of the cutting bar/rod and allow it to sit for approximately 30 seconds. (You will notice that it develops a cloudy appearance.)

6. Burnish the Super-Kote into the full length of the cutting bar/rod. *(Really rub it in.)*

7. Check once more to be sure there is no lighter fluid still on the underside of the cutting bar. After going through all of this effort to get your cutter working so smoothly, you don't want to get a wet mark on the first mat you cut.

That is the entire procedure. It certainly isn't difficult to do and shouldn't take you more than five minutes at most. It will add years to the life of your mat cutter and make your cutting almost effortless. We would be willing to bet that most of you have never had your cutting head move as smoothly or easily.

We have been using this method for about eight years and have found that it does such a good job it no longer becomes necessary to remove the cutting head for additional cleaning. However, whether you have a cutter that has been in use for a while, or a brand new one just out of the box, we would suggest that before you begin regular use of our system you remove the head and give it a very thorough cleaning inside using lighter fluid and cotton swabs. Finish by spraying it liberally with Super-Kote and then burnish it in before replacing it on the rod/cutter bar assembly. This will insure that you get off to a good, clean start.

And as a final note: ***Remember to clean and lubricate your cutter every day before you use it.***

Basic Techniques of Mat Cutting

While this book assumes that you already know how to cut a basic mat, we would like to touch briefly on a few basic techniques you should be familiar with in order to insure good, crisp-looking mats. For those of you who are already doing fine, don't change what you're doing. Remember: "if it works, don't fix it."

- *Your stance at the mat cutter.* Ideally you should position yourself at the base of the mat cutter, reach forward when inserting the blade, and pull smoothly straight toward your body. There are some situations that may arise where you will have to stand more to the side, but at all times try to keep your stroke as straight as possible.

- *Positioning the matboard for cutting.* It is not necessary to place the piece of matboard on which you're working at the bottom of your cutter; you will find it more comfortable if you move it up toward the middle. A position where you will have to lean slightly forward to begin your cutting stroke will automatically cause you to put the right amount of pressure on the handle.

- *Inserting the blade.* To obtain a clean cut, it is of paramount importance to be sure you are using a sharp blade, and that you insert the blade into the matboard smoothly, without jabbing. Keep in mind that the pressure for insertion should come from your *middle* finger not your index finger. You have to control the cutting head and blade at all times. Remember, **slow and smooth**.

- *The Stroke.* The important thing to remember here is to pause briefly after inserting the blade and before starting the stroke. We often see people who are making the insertion and stroke one continuous movement without any pause in between. This can be one of the causes of the dreaded hooks in your mat corners. (We'll have more about hooks later.) For now, remember: **Insert, Pause, Stroke**. After you have practiced this for a while, the pause will be so brief it will seem as if you are doing it all in one motion. That is fine as long as *some* pause is there. If you're not getting quite the cuts you'd like, give this tip a try; we think you'll be pleased with the results.

The key words to remember as you work are **Control** and **Smooth**, and, as always, remember to **Practice**. There is just no substitute for cutting a lot of mats.

Bad Cuts

The title "Bad Cuts" covers a lot of ground. More specifically we're talking about hooks, which are sometimes referred to as "curved corners," ragged edges, and anything else that looks unsightly on your mat.

If we had to pick a single area where framers have the most problems with their mat cutting, it would have to be with hooks. Surprisingly enough, the problem is more often with the operator than with the cutter. While there certainly can be problems with a mat cutter itself, and in particular with older models that have not been properly maintained, those problems are best discussed with your distributor or the manufacturer of your particular machine. We would like to address the operator type of problems and offer some tips that should help to straighten them out for you.

If the truth be known, the majority of hooks in mats are caused by an improper blade depth setting. It is really that simple. There is only one accurate way to set the depth of your blade in the cutting head, and until you do so, you are going to get some degree of a hook.

1. Pick up two pieces of matboard. Any small scraps you have handy will be fine as long as they are of a single thickness and have no other cuts in them. Place both pieces (one on top of the other) under your cutting bar and at any point make a rip cut from end to end.

2. The blade in your cutting head should go through the top piece of board and barely score the piece underneath. Obviously, "barely" is a relative term, but it should go no more than a third to halfway through that second piece. If your blade scores any deeper than that, it is simply out too far. You are using two fresh pieces of matboard so

that you can easily see the score and judge if it is correct or too deep. Once you establish the correct depth for the blade, set the "blade depth adjustment screw" (located at the rear of the blade holder) to insure locating that same position each time you put in a fresh blade.

Knob to Hold Blade in Blade Holder

Blade Depth Adjustment Screw

3. Since matboard varies slightly in thickness from sheet to sheet, you should retest the depth setting periodically using the above method. Remember, you cannot do this accurately by eye.

4. If you cut Alphamat® board or 4-ply rag most of the time, we would recommend you use scraps of those two materials when setting your blade depth. They are slightly different from regular pulp board, so they need their own fine tuning.

If this all seems too simple a solution to hooking problems, keep in mind that those problems are most often caused by a flexing of the blade as it penetrates through the matboard. The less blade there is extending, the less there is to flex. With the blade properly adjusted and the operator concentrating on the "control" we talked about earlier, the corners should come out beautifully.

Another area to check if you're having cutting problems is the slip sheet. (Just for clarification, a slip sheet is a disposable piece of matboard used as an underlayment when cutting your mat.) It is generally felt that slip sheets are necessary to achieve a clean, unragged cut when using the nonjacketed mat cutter blades. All mat cutters produced in this country in the last five years or so take this type of blade. If you're not using a slip sheet and are happy with the results you're getting, just ignore this section. If on the other hand you're not happy with your cuts, try using a slip sheet and compare the results. **Caution:** *It is very important when using a slip sheet to keep it fresh.* Be certain that you don't make a cut in the same track more than once; keep moving the slip sheet around under your cutting bar so that you are working across another cut or into a new area. Slip sheets should be of regular/pulp matboard or Alphamat, rather than 4-ply rag, and should be replaced as often as necessary.

BLADES

Another important consideration in eliminating bad cuts is to be sure you have a sharp blade in the cutter. That may seem a ridiculously obvious statement for us to make, but you would be surprised at how many framers try to stretch the use of their blades through too many mats and end up with bad looking corners. For those who are guilty of this, remind yourself that the cost of a new blade is nothing compared to the irritation and labor cost when you get a bad cut in the middle of a "Creative Mat" and have to start over. The mats you are going to create will be so lovely and will bring in such a good return that it is silly to worry about the cost of changing a blade.

"How many mats should you expect to get out of a single blade?" We cannot answer that question for you exactly. It will depend on a number of things: the type of board you are cutting; how well you have adjusted the depth setting (the farther out a blade is, the faster it dulls); and how smoothly you can make that initial penetration through the matboard. You will also find that some blades or boxes of blades are sharper than others. No one seems to know why, but it's true. If you will try to become very alert to how much drag there is on the blade when you're cutting and how that changes with each cut, it won't take you long to know when to put in a new blade. *If you are ever in doubt, put in a new blade.* Remember, it's better to spend six cents on a new blade than to be forced to resize your mat blanks and start all over again. It's a lot cheaper, too.

Although the nonjacketed blades are available in both 1200 and 1500 thicknesses, we find that the 1200 blade provides a much cleaner and more attractive cut. Because it is thinner it is sharper, and it stands to reason that a sharper blade is going to cut better. As we have discussed earlier, set the blade depth properly, change it regularly, and you will get outstanding results. (The only time we would use a 1500 blade is to cut a mat from something more dense than normal matboard, i.e., chipboard.)

And last, but still so very important, *practice*.

Squaring Up Your Matboard

Before going any further, this is a good time to mention the absolute necessity of squaring up all of your mat blanks. Many framers assume that a sheet of matboard is square when it arrives from the manufacturer or supplier. This is not the case, since manufacturing procedures are not precise enough to consistently yield perfectly square boards.

Because of this, it is important to square up all of your boards while you are cutting them to the required outer dimensions. This is best accomplished by cutting *all four sides rather than just two.* (Obviously, we are assuming that whatever equipment you are using for sizing your board is itself square. If it's not, you will first have to square it up.) Once the machine is square, it is a simple four-step process to square the board.

1. Beginning with any side of the piece of matboard, trim off an inch or so.

2. Turn the board and cut off approximately the same amount from the adjacent side. (Turn the board clockwise each time so that you will be consistent.)

3. Turn the board again and this time cut it to one of the dimensions you require.

4. Turn it a final time and cut the second required dimension for your blank.

If your cardboard and glass cutter, or the "Squaring Arm" on your mat cutter, or whatever you use for sizing board is itself square, you should now have a square mat blank with the outer dimensions that you want.

We might mention that we feel a wall mounted cardboard and glass cutter is the best tool for squaring and sizing board, and there are several brands available in the marketplace. *Just be sure that it is "square" and check it regularly to be sure it stays that way.*

We recommend that you also use the above "squaring up" process when you size a mat from a previous mat "fall out." Theoretically, a "fall out" from a "square" mat blank should be square, but we feel it is best to be sure. Besides it will cut better with the reverse bevels removed. It is a disappointing waste of time and a real profit eater to cut a lovely mat and discover it doesn't fit the artwork properly because it wasn't square to begin with.

2
BASIC CONCEPTS OF CREATIVE MATTING

The "V-Groove"

Your first step on the road to more "Creative Matting" is learning how to cut a basic "V-Groove." It's very easy to do, and will give your mats a real sense of design and style.

1. Begin by selecting any piece of matboard and cutting the outside dimensions to 11" × 14". Set your mat guide on 2", and mark your mat on the back just as you normally would when cutting an ordinary single mat. Now make an arbitrary mark across one of the lines you have drawn. (See Illustration) This is nothing but a reference mark so that you can replace the dropout exactly the same as it was before cutting.

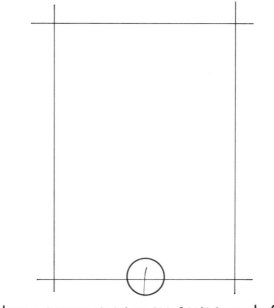

ARBITRARY REFERENCE MARK FOR REPLACEMENT OF CENTER

2. With the matboard marked and referenced, go ahead and cut out your opening. Cut from the back of the board using the guide lines you have drawn as aids to determine where to begin and end each cut. The center will drop out, and you will have an ordinary single mat, just as you have done many times before. Do not discard that center piece, we are going to use it to create our "V-Groove."

3. At this point, move your mat guide over until it is between ⅟₁₆" and ⅛" from the actual cutting bar of your mat cutter. If you have a C & H cutter there is a "V-Groove" stop already there—just move your guide over until it makes contact with the stop and then tighten (see photo below). (This "V-Groove" stop is adjustable on the C & H mat cutter and we'll talk a little later on about how to set it for specific groove widths.) If you are using another brand, they all have provisions for obtaining a "V-Groove" type setting. Check your operating manual.

Mat Guide Moved Over to "V-Groove" Stop

4. *At this time, remove the slip sheet from your mat cutter.* **This is very important.** After removing the slip sheet take the center that you've saved from the mat you cut in step 2 and place it in your mat cutter FACE UP against the mat guide. Trim off all four sides.

5. Take the altered center and put it FACE DOWN on your work table, making note of where the arbitrary reference mark that you made earlier is located.

6. Place the outer mat that you cut out in step 2 on top of the other piece. Be certain to line up the two reference marks.

Mat with "V-Groove"—No Opening Cut

Mat with "V-Groove" and Opening Cut

7. Now tape the two pieces together using Scotch Brand 810 tape. Do not substitute masking tape or anything else, 810 is the one to use.

8. Finally, finish taping the altered center back in securely. Flip it over and you have your first "V-Groove" mat.

9. Complete your mat by setting the guide on 3", mark it, and cut out the opening. You will now have an example of a 3" mat with a "V-Groove" at 2".

Now that you have learned the technique of how to create a "V-Groove," we would like to discuss the two functions that it accomplishes in matting. The first is to *break up space*, and the second is to *add design*. If you take a mat with a 2½" or 3" border and compare it with a mat of the same width and a "V-Groove" somewhere therein, you will immediately see that the groove adds something.

LOCATION OF THE "V-GROOVE"

The actual location of a "V-Groove" in a particular mat is subject to the personal taste of the designer. As is true in almost everything in framing, there is never any one answer for a problem. However, since one of the basic functions of a "V-Groove" is to break up space, we would recommend that you do not put it precisely in the middle. For example:

• In a 2½" mat, we would put the "V-Groove" at 2".

• In a 3" mat, we would put the "V-Groove" at either 1", or at 2", but never at 1½".

However, that is our taste. Remember that there is no one correct solution. Experiment with various placements on your own. The suggestions above will at least give you a couple of places to begin.

> **NOTE: We recommend that you always cut your "V-Groove" in a mat first and then proceed to cut out the opening. There are a couple of exceptions to this which we will discuss and point out individually later on, but unless otherwise specified, always work from the outside border of the mat toward the opening.**

Just for practice, let's cut another 3" mat and this time for variation put the "V-Groove" at 1". You will begin by setting the mat guide on 1"

ADDING DESIGN WITH A "V-GROOVE"

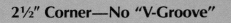

2½" Corner—No "V-Groove"

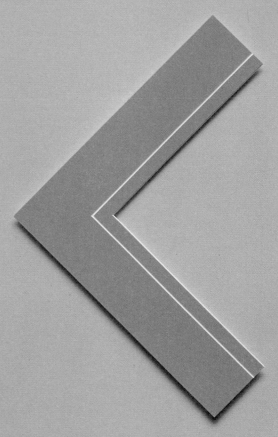

2½" Corner with "V-Groove" at 2"

3" Corner with a "V-Groove" at 1"

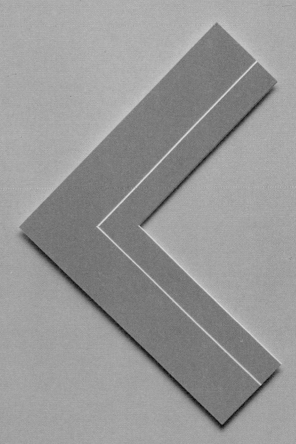

3" Corner with a "V-Groove" at 2"

and then proceed exactly as you did before. This really is not a waste of time, as we want you to get a feel for how the overall look of a mat changes with the position of the "V-Groove." In addition, you will have a couple of different samples to show your customers, which you will need to start selling "V-Groove" mats. Customers have a difficult time visualizing what a finished mat treatment will look like and it is essential to have samples to help them decide.

ADJUSTING THE WIDTH OF THE "V-GROOVE"

We mentioned earlier that the "V-Groove" stop on the C & H cutter is adjustable, and this is a good place to tell you how to make the adjustments. After determining the width of groove you want to use, you will need to obtain a ruler with both millimeter and 64th" markings. Keep in mind that for all practical purposes, the minimum width is ¹⁄₁₆" and the maximum is ⅛" or 3 mm. The stop on the C & H machine comes set from the factory at approximately ¹⁄₁₆", so if you like how the groove looks when it is that narrow, you should just leave it as is. We prefer a groove that is as wide as you can make it, or approximately ⅛". We don't mean to be vague about that measurement, but it can vary slightly from mat cutter to mat cutter. Our feeling is that it becomes more of a design element in a mat when you push it to the wider extreme. (Incidentally, we discovered that maximum totally by experimentation. If you make it any wider, the two pieces will no longer meet at the bottom when taped back together.) The discussion above will hold true as long as the matboard you are cutting is 4-ply or single thick. For other types and thicknesses of board, the width of the "V-Groove" should be adjusted as follows:

- Fabric Mats: ⁹⁄₆₄". This would include linen, suede, and silk matboard. (We have found that it is not possible to execute a "V-Groove" in the grasscloth board.)

- 6-Ply Matboard: ⁷⁄₃₂" or 5 mm

- 8-Ply Matboard: ¹⁰⁄₃₂" or 7 mm

It should be noted that the cutting of 6- and 8-ply matboard is considerably more difficult than the normal 4-ply. However, with practice and *accurate blade depth setting*, it can be accomplished. We feel it

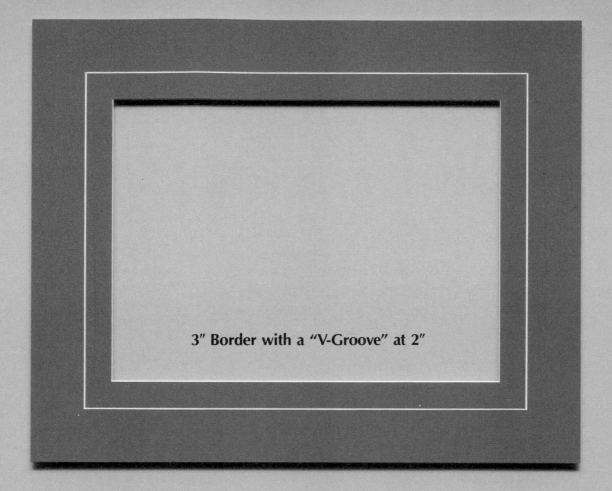

3" Border with a "V-Groove" at 2"

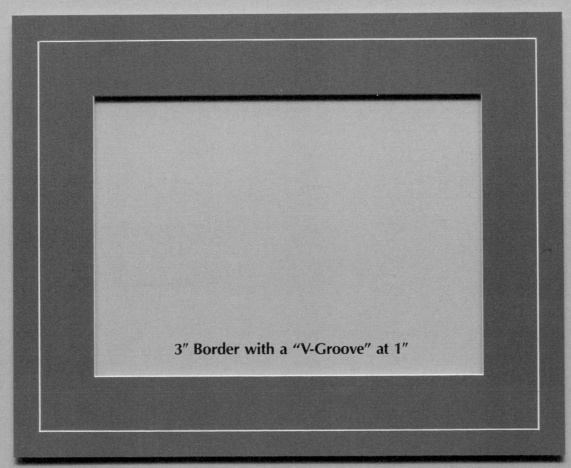

3" Border with a "V-Groove" at 1"

is certainly worth the effort as there are some outstanding effects that can be achieved.

At any rate, whatever the width of groove you decide upon, the method for adjusting the "V-Groove" stop is as follows.

1. Locate the stop on the end of the block to which your mat guide attaches. It is an offset cam about ⅜" from the right side.

2. Move your mat guide over until you make contact with that stop and then tighten it.

3. Place an accurate ruler under the cutter bar on your mat cutter and measure the distance from that bar to the mat guide. This will tell you the width of your groove as the stop is now set.

4. Now loosen the screw in the middle of the offset cam which is your "V-Groove" stop. Offset means that if you rotate this cam clockwise, it will enlarge the setting; counterclockwise, it will make the setting smaller.

5. Make a small adjustment on the cam in the direction you desire and then tighten the screw in the center just slightly. Once again move your guide over until it makes contact with the stop and remeasure the distance from the cutting bar to the guide. If you now have the

"V-Groove" Stop (Offset Cam)

Tightening Screw

Read Ruler Here

Mat Guide Tightening Knob

setting that you want, move your guide out of the way and securely tighten the screw in the middle of the offset cam. If you have not gotten it quite right, make additional adjustments until you do and then tighten the cam securely. The final test will be to execute a "V-Groove" with your new setting and then decide if it has the visual feel that you're after.

Unless you wish to experiment with creating "V-Grooves" of different widths, once you get the stop set correctly there's no reason to move it. There are some interesting mats that we have seen that utilized "V-Grooves" of different widths, but we prefer to use just the one maximum setting. Again, we feel that gives you the most design.

TROUBLESHOOTING BAD GROOVES

If the "V-Groove" stop is set properly and you are not getting clean, accurate grooves, there are a couple of things for you to check and be aware of.

If you find that the width of your groove varies from end to end, it is most likely that your mat guide is out of alignment. This is easy to fix and should be checked regularly as it is crucial for obtaining accurate "V-Grooves" as well as mat openings.

1. Set your mat guide on 2" and tighten it down *only* at the bottom. *Do not* tighten the top screw.

2. Take a fresh scrap of matboard and place it under your cutting bar down near the bottom of the cutter. Draw a pencil line on the board. (See Illustration A on the next page.)

3. Take the same piece of matboard and move it up to the top of your cutter. (Just below the upper guide screw is about right.) Now draw another line on that piece of board. (See Illustration B.) If the two lines do not fall exactly on top of each other, the guide is out of alignment. One tip: It is important to hold your pencil at the same angle to the cutting bar when you are drawing both lines. If you do not, there can be a discrepancy between the two lines that might cause you to think the guide is out of alignment when it really isn't. (See Illustration C.)

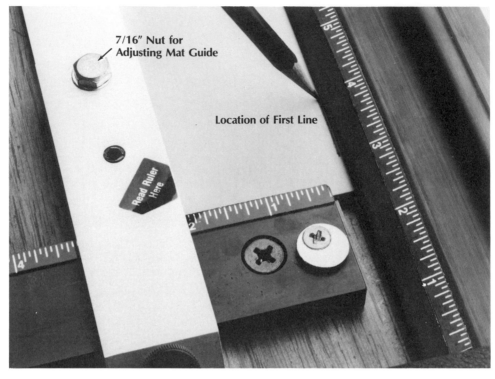

7/16" Nut for
Adjusting Mat Guide

Location of First Line

Read Ruler Here

A

4. To adjust, loosen the 7/16" nut near the bottom of the guide bar and move the bar to the right or left. (See Illustration A again for its location.) The amount and direction will depend on the space between the two lines you drew in steps 3 and 4. Once you have the guide bar back in alignment, retighten the 7/16" nut.

    NOTE: Don't use the scale at the top of the mat cutter to square up your mat guide. You cannot assume that it is absolutely accurate. Use the method that we have just described. Then if the top scale is not "right on," it won't matter. After you set your mat guide at the desired setting and tighten it at the bottom, you will tighten it at the top wherever it falls naturally. Do not try to force it to line up with a specific mark on the upper scale.

    There is another common error that creates problems and prevents you from getting a good looking "V-Groove." We call it "taking a run at the center." The problem occurs when you take the center that you have cut out of your mat and place it back in your cutter face up. (This would be in preparation for removing that small strip of matboard from the four sides that creates your "V-Groove.") If you position the cutting head up above that center and lower your blade and accelerate into the piece of

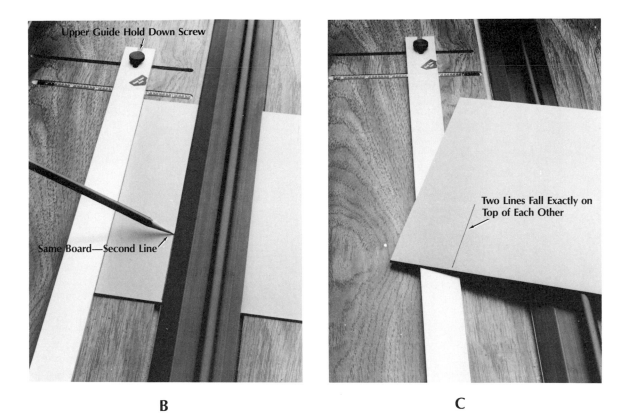

B

C

matboard, you are going to encounter a resistance when the blade makes contact with the piece of matboard. This resistance will usually cause a slight hook and will give your "V-Grooved" center curved corners. This will be extremely noticeable when you tape the two pieces back together.

To avoid this problem, position the cutting head just barely above the center, lower the blade carefully, then slowly and very smoothly move into and down the length of your center. Taking off those little strips should be very controlled and not rushed if you want to avoid the curved corners. While a well-executed "V-Groove" adds a lot of sizzle to a mat, a sloppy one stands out like a sore thumb.

One final note: Always remember to take out your slip sheet before "V-Grooving" the center.

Below we have summarized the four essential techniques that will help you to create beautiful mats every time.

- Control the cutting head at all times.

- Make a smooth penetration through the matboard. Don't jab.

- Use a slow, steady stroke when making your cuts.

- Practice, practice, practice.

31

Double Matting

A double mat is an excellent way to add some extra interest to your framing designs, and it is very easy to do when you use the method known as External Templating. Simply put, you will be using your outside mat as the basis for all your marking. This will hold true no matter how many mats you do, but for now we'll just talk about a double mat.

After you have selected the two mat colors you wish to use, proceed as follows:

1. Determine the width of the border you wish to use on the outer mat and also the amount of color you want on the double or inner mat. We call this the *cuff*. For our example, we are going to use a 3" border on the outer mat and ¼" for the cuff. This will provide us with a total mat width of 3¼" when the double mat is completed.

2. Take a piece of matboard that is the color you want for your outside mat and size it to your required dimensions.

3. Set your mat guide on the amount of border that you want on the outside mat. For our example, it should be set on 3". Now mark the mat blank and cut out your opening. Be sure to save the center that falls out.

4. Now select a piece of matboard that is the color you want for your inside mat. Cut it to a size that is large enough to cover the opening in your outer mat, but smaller than the outside dimension of that mat. While this is an excellent way to use up some of your scrap, don't be too frugal. Be certain that the inner piece is within ½" of the outside dimensions of the outer mat. This will allow for support for a "V-Groove" when used in the outer mat.

5. Put Scotch ATG on all four sides right next to the opening, then tape the second piece on the back of the first. Remember to be certain that no edge of the inner mat piece extends beyond the edge of the outer mat. (See Illustration A on page 34.)

6. Turn over the two pieces that you have taped together and place a *small* piece of ATG in the middle of the inner mat. Place the center that you saved from the outer mat back into the opening and apply some pressure so that it will stick to the ATG tape. (See Illustrations B and C on page 34.)

7. Now *add* the width of the cuff (inner mat) that you want to your first setting on the mat guide. (Remember we had decided to make the border on the outer mat 3″ and that was our first setting on the guide. We had also decided to make the cuff ¼″, so we simply add that amount to our first setting and come up with 3¼″.)

8. Put the two pieces of board that you have already taped together into the cutter, mark your mat, and again cut out the opening. Note that when the center drops out it will be the two pieces of matboard which you taped together.

9. Flip the mat over and you will find a double mat with a 3″ outer mat and a perfect ¼″ cuff all around on the inside. (See Illustration D on page 34.)

If you have been cutting your two mats separately and then trying to line them up by eye, we think you can easily see that this method is a big improvement and much easier. It is so accurate that we often do ¹⁄₁₆″ cuffs on our double and triple mats.

And speaking of cuff widths, we'd like to recommend some combinations that we've found to be aesthetically pleasing in almost any situation. Obviously the width of the cuff in a specific design situation is determined by the effect you wish to create. Just keep in mind that you can introduce or accent almost any color in a piece as long as you use just a little. If your customer is determined to pull out a very strong color in the artwork, suggest a ⅛″, or perhaps a ¹⁄₁₆″, cuff. If it is a safer or less obtrusive color, consider ³⁄₁₆″ or ¼″.

Generally with a 2½″ or 3″ outside mat, we recommend a cuff of either ¼″, ³⁄₁₆″, ⅛″, or ¹⁄₁₆″. A situation may arise where you would want to use more than ¼″ cuff, but it would be unusual.

PROCEDURE FOR USING EXTERNAL TEMPLATING

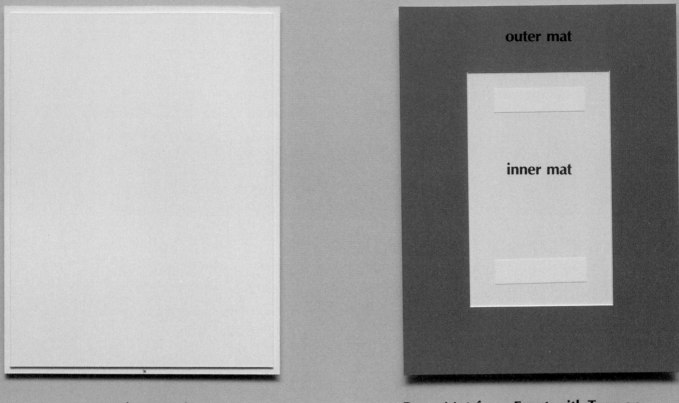

Mat from Back

outer mat

inner mat

B   Mat from Front with Tape on Inner Mat

C   Mat from Front with Center Replaced for Cutting

D   2½″ Border with ¼″ Inner Mat

DOUBLE MATTING: VARIOUS INNER MAT WIDTHS

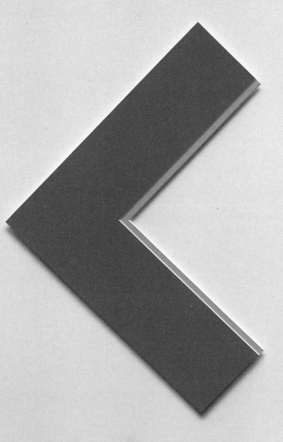

2½″ Border with a ¹⁄₁₆″ Inner Mat

2½″ Border with a ⅛″ Inner Mat

3″ Border with a ³⁄₁₆″ Inner Mat

3″ Border with a ¼″ Inner Mat

Adding a "V-Groove" For Design

Now that you have mastered the double mat, let's talk about spicing up your new skill and adding a "V-Groove" to the design. Since you already know how to execute the groove, we will just point out that it should be cut into your outside mat first, before you cut your opening. Let's use a 3" border again on that outside mat, select a color, and cut the blank to size. Remember that the function of the "V-Groove" is to break up space, so in a 3" mat it should be placed at either 1" or 2". Just for a change and so you can get a feel of what it looks like, let's position it at 1". Having made these preliminary decisions, let's proceed as follows:

1. Set your mat guide on 1". Mark and cut your mat at that setting. Don't forget your reference mark so that the center can be replaced just as it comes out. (Remember at this point we're cutting a "V-Groove.")

2. Move your guide over to the "V-Groove" stop and tighten it down. (Be sure to tighten the screws at both the top and the bottom of the guide.)

3. Put the dropout from step 1 in the mat cutter FACE UP, and remove the small strip from all four sides.

4. Place both pieces of board FACE DOWN on your work surface and line up the reference marks. Before taping them together, turn over your mat and take a look at your groove. Check for ragged edges, small pieces of board in the groove itself, and particularly for any rounded corners where the two pieces might not meet tightly. (Remember to use Scotch 810 tape only.)

5. Set your guide on 3" and mark and cut out your opening.

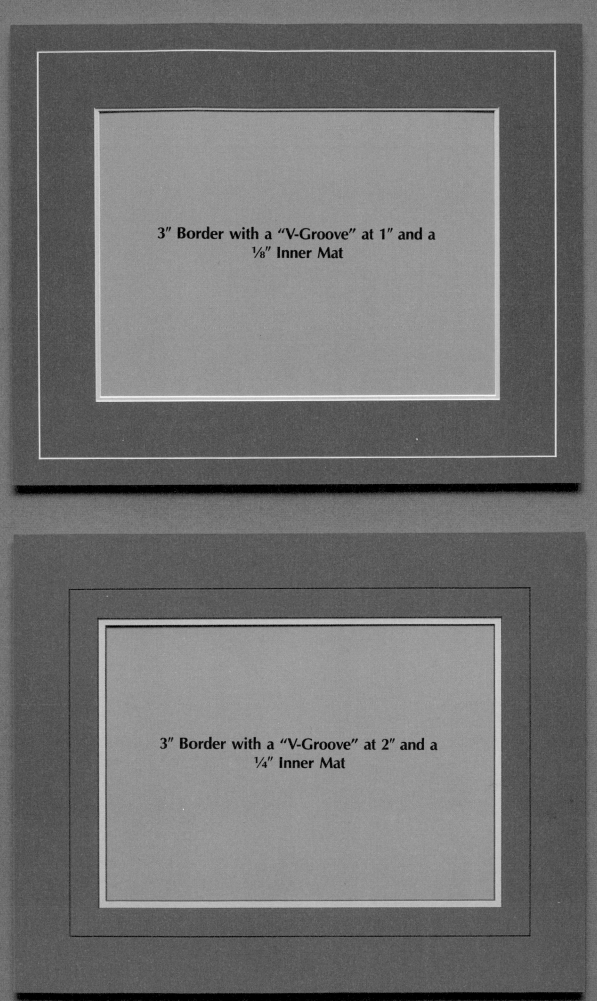

3″ Border with a "V-Groove" at 1″ and a
⅛″ Inner Mat

3″ Border with a "V-Groove" at 2″ and a
¼″ Inner Mat

6. Continue creating the double mat as you did in previous instructions on pages 32–33.

Now you have created a double mat with a "V-Groove," you have something that shows a definitely stylish look. This has become such a basic standard in my shop that we almost never sell anything *less*. You will soon see that there is much more that can be done, but this gives you a start toward creating mats that your customers will begin to notice and admire. It's only a short step from this point to, "Can you mat my picture like that?" It's a proven fact: "Creative Framing" on display sells more framing.

Triple Matting

Once you have explored the possibilities in double matting, the next logical step is to try adding more mats to your design. Toward this end, let's talk about triple matting and some of the really attractive combinations that involve three mats. We have a feeling that the initial reaction from most of you will be "three mats, that's way too much." However, the secret to using several mats is putting them together in the right proportions. To help you get started, we are going to give you some formulas that will work every time. (Triple matting on an 8″ × 10″ piece of artwork might indeed be a little much, so we suggest using these measurements on anything larger than 11″ × 14″.)

- 3, ⅜″, ⅛″: 3″ represents the border on the outside mat, ⅜″ the first cuff, and ⅛″ the innermost cuff. This design provides a total mat width of 3½″.

- 3″, ⅛″, ⅜″: This is a reverse of the cuff dimensions above. It is also a very pleasing combination and immediately gives you a second option to offer your customer.

- 3″, ⅛″, ⅛″: This gives you a total mat width of 3¼″, and is very useful when you want to accent two strong colors in the artwork.

We cannot honestly explain how we arrived at these three formulas. We just kept playing around until we found what we thought looked good. Later on, after applying them to hundreds of framing problems, we realized that they worked every time. We're sure that as you practice and experiment you will find other combinations you like; but use these to get started. Prove to yourself and to your customers that triple matting can indeed be tasteful. And not to be ignored, *profitable*. (A triple mat will be three times as expensive as a single mat.)

Keep in mind that you're going to need samples of all these techniques in order to sell them. It is imperative to have several corner samples of triple mats in order to help your customers visualize the finished product. Even if you don't have a sample in the particular color combination they want to use, you need to show them the proportions and how the three colors will work together. As you practice, make corner samples that you can use later as selling tools.

As far as the actual execution of a triple mat, you already know how to do it. Proceed as you did with your double mat, and just take it one step farther.

1. Pick the three colors of matboard that you want to use. Cut the outer mat to your required dimensions.

2. Set your guide on 3", mark, and cut out the opening. Save the dropout.

3. Tape the matboard for your second mat on the back of the outer mat. Remember, the second piece must be big enough to cover the opening but not as big as the outside dimensions of the first mat. Tape the dropout from the first mat back in. Move the guide to 3⅜", mark, and cut out the opening. (We added the width of the cuff to our first guide setting of 3".) Mark and cut out the second mat. Save the dropout again. This time it will be the two centers that are taped together.

4. Now tape the matboard for your third mat on the back of the first two mats you have cut. Again, this piece must be big enough to cover the opening but not extend over the outer limits of the first mat. Actually, we usually make the pieces for the two cuffs the same size. Tape the two dropouts from step 3 back in. Move your mat guide to 3½", mark, cut out the third opening, and you have a good looking triple mat.

Just as with a double mat, this design can be jazzed up even more by adding a "V-Groove." *You know how to do it, just remember that the groove is cut into the outer mat before the opening.* In this 3" border you will have a choice of positioning it at either 1" or 2".

Appendix B lists a number of triple mat color combinations that we have found to have widespread applications. We hope that you will find them useful.

TRIPLE MATTING COMBINATIONS

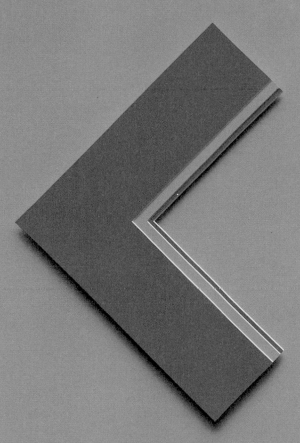

3″ Border—³⁄₈″ and ¹⁄₈″ Inner Mats

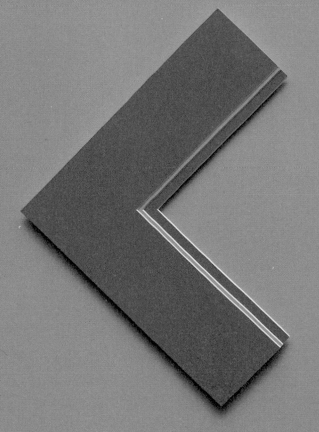

3″ Border—¹⁄₈″ and ³⁄₈″ Inner Mats

3″ Border—Two ¹⁄₈″ Inner Mats

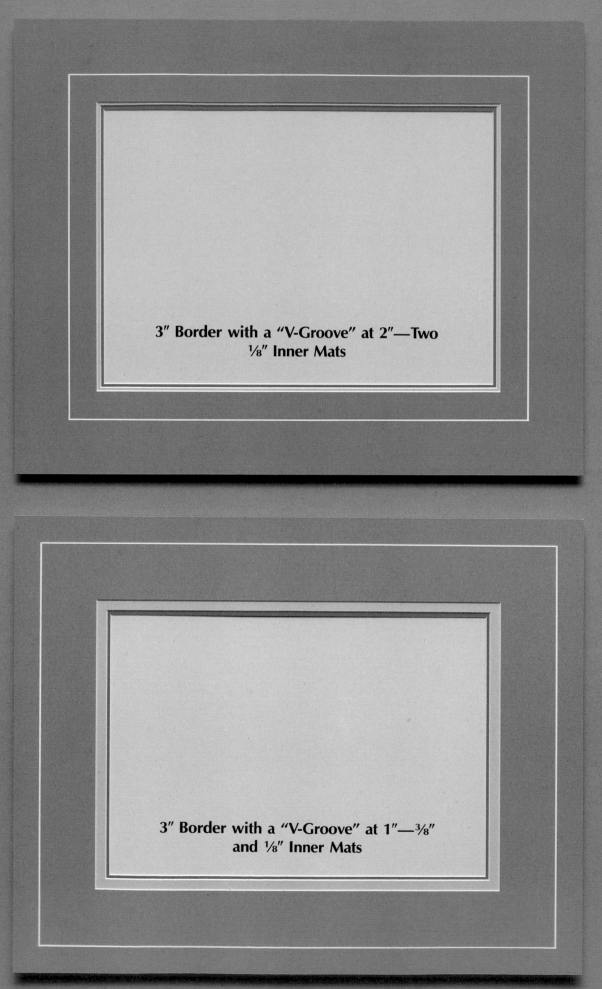

3" Border with a "V-Groove" at 2"—Two
⅛" Inner Mats

3" Border with a "V-Groove" at 1"—⅜"
and ⅛" Inner Mats

The Inlay Mat

For those of you who may not know what an inlay mat is, let's begin with a brief description. It is simply a method of laying pieces of matboard together to provide two or more colors in a mat with only *one* thickness of matboard. This is the opposite effect of double or triple matting, which provides for multiple colors by stacking boards on top of each other. While the inlay mat is not used as often as it once was, it is a skill you definitely should develop. For the customer who wants nonglare glass and a double mat, it is really essential. As you know, nonglare glass has a tendency to soften colors when separated from the artwork by more than one thickness of matboard. In addition, there are some great effects that can be achieved combining an inlay mat with one or more "V-Grooves."

We are going to give you two methods of achieving an inlay mat. While both ways give you the same end result, you may find that you're more comfortable with one method than the other. For the first method, you must use a slip sheet on your first cut whether you normally do or not. This is important. If you fail to do this, you will find that you will not have a tight fit when you tape the two inlaid pieces together. So, having warned you, let's do our first inlay.

THE INLAY MAT—METHOD ONE

1. Select a piece of matboard and cut it to size. At the same time choose a second piece for your inlay color. This is the board you are going to "inlay" into the first. Just as when we were working on double and triple mats, this second piece should be slightly smaller

than the outside dimensions of the first piece. (Caution: It should not be much smaller. About ½″ on each side is perfect.)

2. For our example, we will use a 2½″ border and elect to place our inlay at 2⅛″. This will make our inlay ⅜″ wide. As soon as you have made these decisions, you are ready to begin. We will talk about design later, after you have learned how to cut the inlay.

3. *Remember, this step requires the use of a slip sheet.* Now set your mat guide on 2⅛″. This is where you're going to inlay the second color into the first. Using the matboard color for the outer border, mark it, and cut out the opening. You will not need to save this dropout.

4. Using a *small* piece of ATG tape on all four sides, attach the board for your inlay color to the back of the mat you cut in step 3. This is no different from when you were doing a double mat.

5. *Do not move your mat guide,* but *remove* the slip sheet. Put the two boards that you taped together into the mat cutter and make a rip cut on all four sides. (A rip cut means cutting from top to bottom of the mat without any guide lines.) As long as your blade depth is properly adjusted, it will not go through both mats. Please refer to our previous discussion on setting blade depth if that should occur. Before you separate the center, make a reference mark so that it can be properly aligned with the initial mat.

6. After completing the rip cuts and peeling the strips away, take the center that remains and tape it into the opening of your first mat. Be sure to check your reference mark for proper alignment and to use Scotch 810 tape. *Tip*: You will notice that there is ATG tape still on the back of your mat, and unless removed, it will be sticking to everything and making a mess. The easy way to take it off is to place a piece of masking tape over the ATG; when you pull the masking tape off, it will take the ATG with it. This saves a lot of wear and tear on your thumb.

   Now flip your mat over. You should find two colors with only one matboard thickness and the pieces fitting tightly together with no gaps.

7. Finally, move your guide to 2½″; mark your mat and cut out the opening. This will complete your inlay mat. It has two colors of board with only one thickness, and has a 2½″ border with a ⅜″ wide inlay at 2⅛″. And it looks terrific—CONGRATULATIONS!

INLAY MAT

**3″ Border with ⅜″ Inlay at 2″ and a ⅛″
Inner Mat**

Once you have grown comfortable with these steps for executing an inlay mat, you can move on to learn some extras that will add even more interest and design. However, before doing that, we want to give you our second method for cutting the inlay.

THE INLAY MAT—METHOD TWO

The first two steps in both methods are identical, but we will repeat them here so you will not have to flip back and forth between pages.

1. Select a piece of matboard and cut it to size. At the same time choose a second piece for your inlay color. This second piece should be slightly smaller than the outside dimensions of the first piece.

2. For this example we will again be using a 2½" border with a ⅜" inlay at 2⅛".

3. Take the two colors of matboard that you have selected and *begin* by joining them together with ATG on all four sides. (Remember, in the other method you actually cut the opening in the first piece of board *before* joining them together.)

4. Set your mat guide on 2½" and mark the back of the board sandwich you created in step 3. **Be certain that you have removed the slip sheet from your cutter** and then go ahead and cut out the opening you've marked. (Just as with our first method, if your blade depth is properly adjusted it will not cut through both mats.)

5. After cutting, *do not* separate the two pieces but immediately move your mat guide to 2⅛" and rip cut all four sides. Be certain to make a reference mark for later alignment and then peel off the strips. Gently put the mat you have just created aside; this is your inlay. (Note: The opening is already cut out.)

6. *Leaving the guide set as it is, replace the slip sheet into your cutter,* mark, and cut out the opening in the remaining piece of matboard.

7. Line up your reference marks and securely tape the inlay piece from step 5 into the opening you cut out in step 6. This completes the steps for our alternate method and also gives you a 2½" mat with a ⅜" inlay at 2⅛".

We do want to emphasize that neither method is better than the other, and while both will provide fine inlay mats, most framers will have a favorite. For instance, although I like to use the first method, Val prefers the latter. We encourage you to try them both before making your decision.

Beyond the Basic Inlay Mat

In this section we are going to show you three different ideas that will add a little something *extra* to your inlay mats. None of these will alter the basic technique for doing the inlay but will require a few additional steps to get the end result.

ADDING A "V-GROOVE" BETWEEN THE TWO INLAID COLORS

Method One

1. Begin by executing steps 1–5 of the procedure for cutting the basic inlay mat. (Please refer to pages 43–44.)

6. After completing the rip cuts and peeling the strips away, take the inlay piece that you have created and "V-Groove" it. (You should have made a reference mark while you were executing the steps for an inlay, and that will indicate how to align the piece after it has been grooved. As always, be certain that it is taped in securely.)

7. Complete the mat by setting your mat guide on 2½", mark it, and cut out your opening.

By "V-Grooving" the inlay color *before* taping it back in, you will have created an inlay mat with a "V-Groove" between the two colors. It has a great look and as you can see is very easy to do. Now let's go through the execution of the identical mat using our alternate method.

Method Two

1. This time begin by executing steps 1–4 of the alternate method for cutting inlays (page 46).

5. After cutting out the opening in step 4, *do not* separate the two pieces but move your mat guide to 2⅛″ and make rip cuts on all four sides. *Before* peeling up the strips, place Scotch 811 (removable) tape over the opening cuts that you made. This is done to insure that the center will not drop out, for we will need its support for our next step of "V-Grooving" the inlay piece. As always, be certain to make a reference mark for later alignment of the inlay. *Now* peel up your strips.

6. Take care that the center remains intact and set the inlay piece aside.

7. *Replace the slip sheet into your cutter* and leave your mat guide set on 2⅛″. Mark and cut out the opening in your bottom matboard.

8. Take the inlay piece that you put aside in step 6 and "V-Groove" it. Upon completion of the cutting, remove the Scotch 811 tape and drop out the center you cut in step 4.

9. Line up your reference marks and securely tape the pieces together. This will complete your mat.

Whichever method you decide to use, you have now created an inlay mat with a "V-Groove" between the two colors. Be sure to compare it with the basic inlay mats that you completed. Notice that each has a slightly different effect and store them away for your future use.

We do want to emphasize that the Scotch 811 tape, which is removable, is not a substitute for the Scotch 810. The 810 is permanent and should always be used when assembling mats to be installed in frames. 811 is used only when temporary holding is necessary during the execution of a particular mat design.

ADDING A "V-GROOVE" WITHIN THE INLAID COLOR

Method One

1. For this design you will need three pieces of matboard: two pieces that are the same color and a third piece of a different color for your inlay. Begin by following steps 1–6 from the beginning discussion

on the Inlay mat (pages 43–44). However, please note that this time we are using a 3" border, and will be placing a ⅜" wide inlay at 2" in that border. (This means your first setting on the guide will be at 2" rather than 2⅛".)

7. After you have completed steps 1–6, you should have one color inlaid into the other at 2". Proceed by moving your mat guide to 2³⁄₁₆" and again marking the same mat. We are going to execute a "V-Groove" at this setting, so do not forget the reference mark for replacing the center dropout properly.

8. Cut out the opening, "V-Groove" the dropout, and tape it back in. Be sure that the center is securely taped with Scotch 810. If there is any confusion with this step, refer back to cutting a basic "V-Groove" (pages 21–24).

9. Now move your guide to 2⅜" and repeat steps 3–6 once again. For this inlay, you will be using a piece of board that is the same color as the one you started with. Be particularly careful to tape it back together securely.

10. Finish your mat by moving the guide to 3" and cutting out the opening.

Upon completion you will have a 3" mat with an inlay at 2" which is ⅜" wide, and a "V-Groove" in the middle of the inlay.

Method Two

If you decide to use this method, you will need to select only two pieces of matboard (one of each color) rather than the three that method one requires.

Once again, we will be using a 3" border with a ⅜" inlay at 2" and there will be a "V-Groove" in the middle of that inlay. When you have selected your colors, cut one board to whatever outside dimensions you have decided on and then cut the second piece slightly smaller. This is no different than the beginning steps for a basic inlay mat. As soon as you have sized your matboard, proceed as follows:

1. *Put the slip sheet into your cutter* and set your mat guide on 2⅜". Mark and cut the larger of your two pieces of matboard, but be careful *not* to let the center fall out. (Once again, you will want to use the Scotch 811 removable tape.)

INLAY MATS

2½″ Border with ⅜″ Inlay at 2⅛″

3″ Border with ⅜″ Inlay at 2″

2½″ Border with
⅜″ Inlay at 2⅛″ and a
"V-Groove" between Colors

3″ Border with ⅜″ Inlay at 2″ and
"V-Groove" at 2³⁄₁₆″ within Inlay Color

3″ Border with ⅜″ Inlay at 2″ and
"V-Grooves" on Either Side of Inlaid Color

2. Using ATG on all four sides, tape your second board to the back of the one you just finished cutting.

3. *Remove the slip sheet from your cutter*, but *do not* move the mat guide. Place the two boards that you stuck together in step 2 into the cutter, mark, and cut out an opening. As soon as you finish, put Scotch 811 (the removable tape) over the cuts to prevent the center from falling out.

4. Now move the mat guide to 2″ and, being careful not to separate the boards, make the rip cuts. After making a reference mark for future alignment, peel off the strips and put this piece aside gently.

5. *Put the slip sheet back into the cutter*, but *do not* move your mat guide. Using the outer piece of matboard from step 1, mark it and cut out an opening.

6. Take the inlay piece that you created in step 3 and tape it securely into the opening cut in step 4. Be careful that the center does not fall out (remember you taped it with 811) and use your reference marks for accurate alignment.

7. Taking the pieces you taped together in step 5, set your mat guide on 2³⁄₁₆″, mark it, and cut out an opening. "V-Groove" the center that drops out, then tape it back in securely. (Because of all the pieces we are dealing with in this mat, it is very important that they are all put back together carefully. Any shifting around could affect your accuracy, and you do not want a sloppy looking inlay. And, after all of this effort, you certainly do not want any pieces to separate at a later date in the frame.)

8. Remove the Scotch 811 and let the center fall out of the piece you just finished "V-Grooving."

9. Remove the Scotch 811 that is holding your center dropout from step 1 and tape that center in place of the one you took out in step 7. (This last piece will be the same color as the outer border of your mat.)

10. After making sure that everything is well taped, complete the mat by moving your mat guide to 3″ and cutting out the opening.

Although some of the inlay mat terminology may sound a little complicated, it won't take long for you to get the hang of it. Be sure to save this sample (and all the others that you make) to show your customers and as a reference for you and other framers in your shop. If you wish, make notes right on the back of it—these may well come in handy the next time you do this particular cut.

ADDING TWO "V-GROOVES," ONE ON EITHER SIDE OF THE INLAY

Method One

For this example, we will again use a 3" border and will put a ⅜" wide inlay at 2". In addition, there will be a "V-Groove" on either side of that inlay.

1. Just as for our second inlay variation, you will need three pieces of matboard: one that is the outer border color, a second of a different color for the inlay, and a third that is the same color as the first. The second and third piece will be slightly smaller than the outside dimensions of the first. Since we are going to inlay at 2", that will be our first mat guide setting.

2. *Insert a slip sheet into the cutter.* Mark the board that is cut to your desired outer dimensions and cut out an opening. After cutting it, attach the board that is your inlay color on the back with ATG.

3. *Do not move your mat guide, but remove the slip sheet from your cutter.* Take the two boards that you stuck together in step 2 and make rip cuts on all four sides. Peel the strips off and remove any residue of ATG from the back of the outer mat.

4. "V-Groove" the inlay piece that you created in step 3 above. Tape it securely into the outer mat border.

5. *Once again, replace the slip sheet into your cutter*, and move the mat guide to 2⅜".

6. Repeat steps 2–4 above. When you reach step 3, you will use the third piece of matboard that you sized before beginning. (This will be the same color as the outside border.)

7. To complete the mat, move your guide to 3", mark, and cut out the opening.

You now have an inlay mat with a "V-Groove" on either side of the inlaid color. This really does have great style; we have used it frequently. We will caution you one more time to tape everything back together securely.

If you prefer method two for executing inlay mats, you should have no problem in using it to cut this design. Just follow the instructions we gave you for the second "extra" (pages 50–52) and "V-Groove" each of the pieces before you tape them back in. When referring back to those steps, remember to leave out the third "V-Groove" at 2³⁄₁₆"—it could get a little busy. Or, you might want to give it a try just to see how it looks. We have come up with many of our best designs by playing around like that.

As you compare this last with all the other mats you have completed involving the inlay, keep in mind that no one of them is any better than the other. They are all creative and interesting. The final decision of which one to use is between you and your customer. Although we are really just getting started, you have already developed quite a bag of tricks to show your clients. For those of you who have galleries, do not wait until you can sell some of these ideas to a framing customer. Use them in designing pieces that belong to you and get them out where people can see them. "Creative framing" will help you to merchandise your artwork and along the way will also sell more (and more expensive) framing. Give it a try; it really works.

Creating
a Window Effect

One of the easiest and most effective methods of creating visual interest in your matting is to use what we call a Window Mount. All this involves is creating a spacer between your mat, or mats, and the artwork. This is easily done by cutting a mat out of a piece of 3/16" foam core board that has the exact same outer dimensions as your mat. Proceed as follows:

1. After sizing the foam core, set your mat guide for 1/4" less than the opening of your mat. (If your mat is 3", your guide would be set on 2¾".)

2. At that setting cut the opening out of the piece of foam core just as if it were a piece of matboard. *Please note:* Due to the 3/16" thickness of the foam core board, it will be necessary to extend your blade for this cut. You will have to do a little experimenting to find the right amount. *Be certain that you have a slip sheet under the foam core and that you do not extend the blade so far that it cuts into your mat cutter base.* You don't need to be concerned with hooks, overcuts, or undercuts on this mat; they are not going to show.

3. Put ATG tape on the back of the *foam core mat* on all four sides right next to the opening.

4. Flip your foam core mat over so that the bevel goes back away from the opening of the matboard mat. (This will make the spacer virtually invisible, and your matting will appear to float above the artwork.) Align the outer edges of the two mats and apply pressure so as to join them together. Flip it right side up and you are all done.

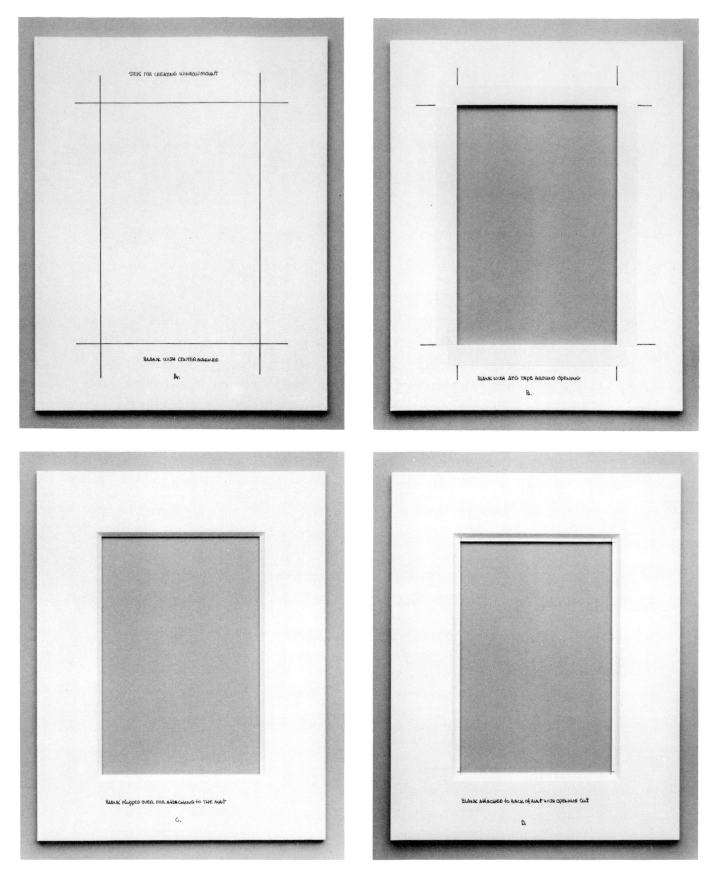

STEPS FOR CREATING WINDOW MOUNT

BLANK WITH CENTER MARKED

A.

BLANK WITH ATG TAPE AROUND OPENING

B.

BLANK FLIPPED OVER FOR ATTACHING TO THE MAT

C.

BLANK ATTACHED TO BACK OF MAT WITH OPENING CUT

D.

VARIOUS WINDOW EFFECTS

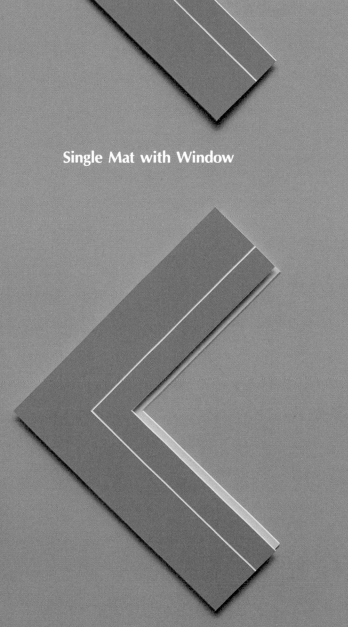

Single Mat with Window

Double Mat with Window

Double Mat with Window between the Mats

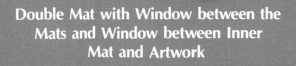

Double Mat with Window between the Mats and Window between Inner Mat and Artwork

Although the foam core board does come in three different thicknesses (⅛", ³⁄₁₆", and ⅜"), we have found that the ³⁄₁₆" is what we use 90 percent of the time. The ⅛" just does not provide enough depth to justify the effort and, while we have occasionally used the ⅜", it is just one more material to keep in stock. Please do give all three thicknesses a try, though, and make your own decisions.

Within the last year or so, the foam core board has also become available in an acid free format. This enables you to use this very effective technique when doing conservation framing. In fact, a single 4-ply rag board with a "V-Groove" and a Window Mount is a very elegant and clean looking presentation. It's a real "Museum look"—give it a try.

There are a number of variations on the Window Mount technique, all of which can be used very effectively. We suggest that you give each of the following a try (see photos on page 57).

- A single mat with a Window Mount

- A double mat with a Window Mount

- A double mat with a Window Mount between the two mats

- A double mat with a Window Mount under the top mat and another Window Mount under the inner mat

When designing with Window Mounts, be certain that the frame you choose has enough depth to accommodate them. (The last mat described above would require a rabbet depth of at least ¾".) We have found the metal mouldings (Nielsen® Profile #22 or 71) to be quite versatile with this technique.

And again, make up some sample Window Mount corners that you can use when working on frame designs with your customers. In addition to these working samples, this is one technique that will really pay off when shown in your framed artwork display. We absolutely guarantee that it will bring reactions and increased framing sales.

General Discussion on Pricing

One of the most important topics we intend to discuss in this text is *pricing*. While it's great to learn "creative" cuts and how to use them in designing your mats, it is absolutely essential that you know how to charge for them. If you cannot get a fair return for these new skills of yours, you're not going to be too anxious to sell them to your customers. We are well aware that there are individual factors that have to be considered by each framer when establishing pricing. These would include locale, population, and competition. However, what each reader must understand is that once you have assimilated the material in this volume, you will no longer be charging your customer for time and materials, but rather for "creativity" and "design." Not only will those customers be excited about the work that you do for them, but they will also understand and accept the charges for this "design" ability. The first thing you have to do is to start thinking of yourself as a "Mat Designer" and then remember not to be afraid of charging for your "creativity."

Keep in mind that all the pricing we are going to give you is nothing but a guideline. You are going to have to make your own final judgment about what to charge for specific techniques. Don't assume that your customers will not pay for "Creative Matting." If you show them samples of what you can do, we are sure you will be pleasantly surprised. Whatever your decision is about pricing, be sure to charge something. You must not give away your design skills.

Our pricing system is based on what is known as the *united inch*. It's the method that we use for arriving at a charge for the matboard and any "V-Groove" or "V-Grooves" that we might use in that particular mat. For those of you who are not familiar with this term, the number of united inches in a mat (or frame for that matter) is determined by totaling the number of inches in two adjacent sides. For example:

an 8″ × 10″ mat = 18 united inches

If you are dealing with a mat that involves a fractional size, simply round off to the next higher inch. For example:

a 28¾″ × 38⁹⁄₁₆″ mat = 68 united inches (29 + 39)

It is really that simple; first determine the number of united inches in your mat, and then multiply that figure times the charge per united inch for whatever creative technique you plan to use.

Just to get started, let's determine per united inch prices for the things we have already discussed. Once again, these will be what *we* charge for the techniques and are for you to use only as guidelines in making your own decisions. In the past ten years, we have taught hundreds of students and given many seminars on "Creative Matting," all of which have included discussion on pricing. So there are many framers out there who are already charging and getting a good return for their matting. Please do give it a try.

NOTE: All of our suggested pricing is current and valid at the time of publication of this text (September 1987). The authors cannot be responsible for future cost increases in materials and/or overhead expenses and do not guarantee a profit margin from any of the techniques discussed.

RECOMMENDED UNITED INCH PRICING

Regular or Paper matboard—.10 to .12 per united inch

Black Core matboard—.20 per united inch

Alphamat or Alpharag board—.30 united inch

Fabric Matboards:
    Linen—.80 per united inch
    Suede—$1.00 per united inch
    Silk—$1.00 per united inch

"V-Grooves":
> Regular—.15 united inch

Multiple matting should be the sum of the united inch charges for the types of board used:
> Double mat (Alphamat)—.60 united inch
> Triple mat (Alphamat)—.90 united inch

"V-Grooves" with Multiple Mats:
> Double mat with "V-Groove" (Alphamat)—.75 united inch (.60 + .15)
> Triple mat with "V-Groove" (Alphamat)—$1.05 united inch (.90 + .15)

Window Mounts:
> Regular foam core—.20 united inch
> Acid free foam core—.30 united inch

Inlay mats:
> Single inlay (Alphamat)—.60 united inch (same as for a double mat)
> Double inlay (Alphamat)—.90 united inch (same as for a triple mat)
> Inlay mats with a "V-Groove"—same as above charges plus .15 united inch/per groove

As you can see, all the charges are cumulative. Every time you do something extra to the mat blank, you can get additional return for it. Although we have included a recommended charge for paper mat or regular pulp board, we have to admit that we use only 4-ply rag or Alphamat in our framing business. In addition to the conservation qualities, which are so important, most of our customers have come to request it even if their artwork does not require it. They really like the look of the white bevel and, in particular, the extra crisp look of the "V-Groove." However, because it makes such a strong "design" statement, we do feel that the Black™ by Bainbridge board should be an essential part of your "bag of tricks." You must be aware that it is not conservation quality/museum standard and should not be used in matting valuable artwork.

We do want to emphasize once again that we are not trying to sell you anything. Just keep in mind that all the techniques in this book can be done in any kind of matboard that you may choose to work with, and always remember that there is more profit in matting than anything else we handle in framing. The only thing that limits how much return you can get out of a sheet of matboard is what you do to it. Just to give you an example; using the united inch pricing formulas that we have given you, a double Alphamat with one regular "V-Groove" in 22½" × 30¼" would price as follows:

22½" × 30¼" = 54 united inches
At .30/united inch for each Alphamat = .60/united inch, *plus* .15/united inch for the regular "V-Groove," we have a total cumulative charge of .75/united inch.
Multiply 54 united inches × .75 /united inch, and we get a total mat charge of $40.50.

That certainly is enough to justify the small amount of extra time it takes to cut that particular mat.

We have spent a great deal of time thinking about the pricing problem and are convinced that using a united inch method is the only way for the framer to get an easily adjustable and fair return for his or her time and creativity while designing and cutting mats. We all know that it's more difficult and time consuming to cut a "V-Groove" in a matboard that's 30" × 40" than one that's 8" × 10". This method of pricing will compensate you for that fact.

We're sure that many readers will be at least slightly astonished at the charge we gave for the 54 united inches mat above. If you are one of those, we would like to point out that our system also takes into account one final factor that many framers often forget: the time it takes to come to a design decision with your customer. As we all know, it can be time consuming and therefore bite heavily into your profit. Using the united inch method for your pricing will cover you on all the hidden profit-eating parts of the mat design and cutting processes. Knowing that you are getting a good return for being "creative" goes a long way toward providing the incentive to spend extra time in designing and cutting your mats.

Now that we have given you some basic thoughts on pricing and the united inch charges for the techniques discussed up to this point, we will be indicating a recommended charge for each new technique as it is presented. For a quick reference you will find a Pricing Summary covering all the techniques and designs discussed in the book in Appendix A.

Offset Corners

Offset Corners are an easy way to add a little something extra to your mats. They can be accomplished as follows:

1. Determine the width of the border you wish to use. (Let's use 2½" for our example.) Set your mat marking guide on the width you have selected. Mark your blank. (See Diagram A on page 64.)

2. Now move your guide to 2¾" and again mark your mat. It is a good idea to mark with a red pencil this time. It will make it easier to keep everything straight until you get comfortable with executing this corner. (See Diagram B.)

3. At this same setting, cut from red circle to red circle as marked in Diagram B.

4. Move your guide back to your initial setting of 2½" and cut from black circle to black circle as marked in Diagram C. This will complete your offset corner mat.

In our opinion, this corner looks better with a "V-Groove" in your mat, and the recommended placement would be at 2". However, do not be afraid to experiment with that. There is never any one solution, and you may find something that you like better.

LAYOUT FOR OFFSET CORNERS

LAYOUT FOR OFFSET CORNERS

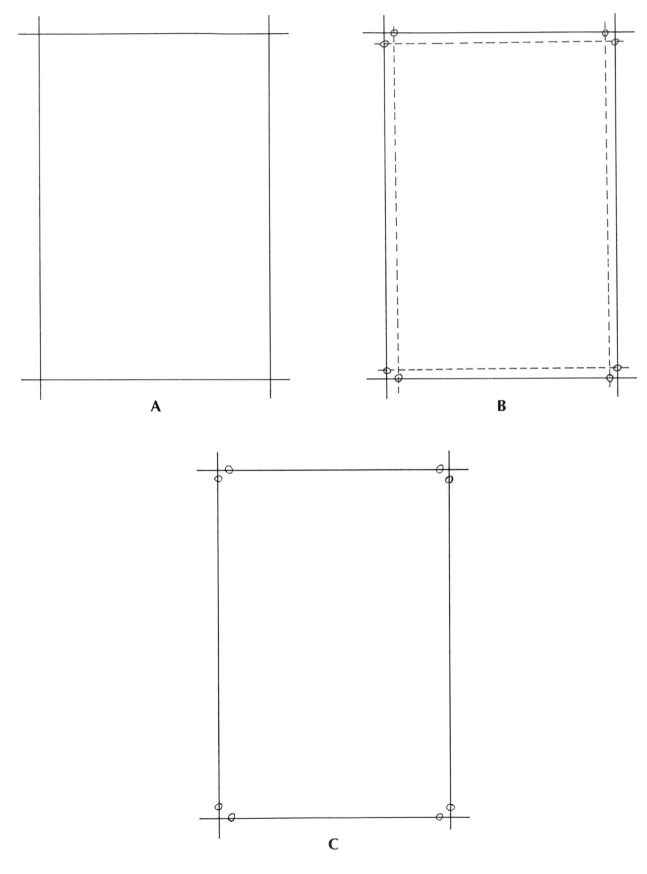

A

B

C

USING THE "V-GROOVE" WITH OFFSET CORNERS

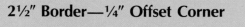

2½″ Border—¼″ Offset Corner

2½″ Border—¼″ Offset Corner with "V-Groove" at 2″

3″ Border—⅜″ Offset Corner with "V-Groove" at 1″

3″ Border—½″ Offset Corner with "V-Groove" at 2″

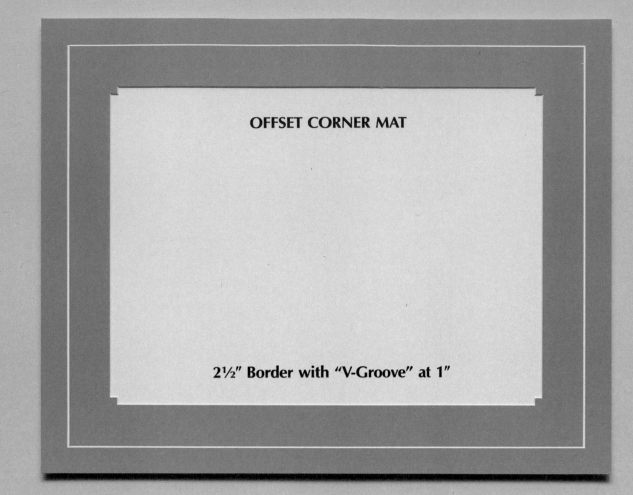

OFFSET CORNER MAT

2½″ Border with "V-Groove" at 1″

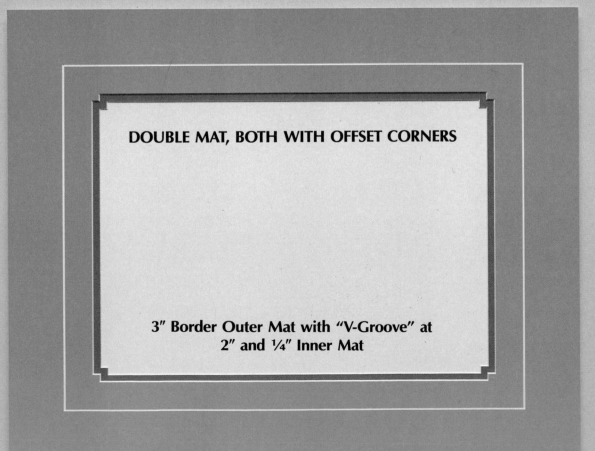

DOUBLE MAT, BOTH WITH OFFSET CORNERS

3″ Border Outer Mat with "V-Groove" at 2″ and ¼″ Inner Mat

SUGGESTED PRICING: Offset Corners are $4.00/mat *plus* your regular charge for the board and the charge for a "V-Groove" if used. Please refer to the pricing section for recommended united inch charges on these.

VARIATIONS ON OFFSET CORNERS

Once you have learned how to execute an Offset Corner mat, it is a good idea to do some experimenting with different offsets, in order to get a visual feel for how they will look. At the very least we recommend that you make a sample of a ⅜" and a ½" Offset Corner mat. It will give you additional practice in creating this corner and provide some samples as selling tools. Many customers have a difficult time visualizing these more "creative" corners; they really need to *see* them.

As for double mats with Offset Corners, they are best accomplished by sizing the two pieces of matboard you are going to use to an identical size and then cutting them separately. We feel that you will get the best results using this method, and there is really no problem as long as you get both pieces of matboard *exactly* the same size.

SUGGESTED PRICING: The charge for a double Offset Corner mat would be the same as a regular double mat *plus* $4.00/mat for the Offset Corners and an additional .15/united inch if you use a "V-Groove."

3

MORE ADVANCED CONCEPTS

As we begin to discuss the more advanced techniques of "Creative Matting," we cannot emphasize too much the importance of making samples of everything. It is impossible to sell this kind of matting without examples to show your customers, and while corner samples will certainly help, the more finished artwork you can get up on your walls the easier sales will be. After fifteen years of owning a gallery/frameshop, I have learned that attractive, well designed, and "creative" framing will help you to merchandise your artwork and will in turn also sell more of your framing. Customers have no idea of how "creative" you can be unless you show them with the artwork hung in your display space. Take some of the inventory that belongs to you, and forgetting about budget, design the best and most "creative" framing you possibly can. It doesn't matter if you end up with $200.00 worth of framing on a $25.00 print, as long as the finished product looks like it is worth $225.00. If a customer comes into your shop and loves it, he or she is not going to ask you how much of the cost is artwork, and how much is framing. He or she will buy it as an entity; and that is merchandising with your framing. Even if customers don't care for that particular piece, the chances are very good that they will notice your special framing and want something of theirs framed that same way.

The Slant Corner Opening Mat

What we are about to discuss is the foundation upon which everything else in this volume will be built and, as such, it is extremely important. Please keep working with this section until you are totally comfortable with the Slant Corner Concept and certain that you understand it.

After cutting a mat blank to size, a Slant Opening mat will be achieved by the following steps. For this first practice mat, cut your blank to 11″ × 14″.

SLANT CORNER OPENING—PRACTICE MAT ONE

1. After deciding how wide a border you would like to use (let's use 2½″ for this sample), put your mat guide on that setting. **Important:** *When executing a Slant Corner mat, the first setting for your guide will always be the location where you want that slant corner in your mat.* We intend to use 2½″, and with the guide at that setting, mark your mat in the usual way. (See Diagram A on page 72.)

2. You must now decide how much of a slant corner you would like to have and add that amount to the setting on your mat guide from step 1. Let's start out with a ⅜″ slant corner, so our second setting on the guide will be 2⅞″. (We added ⅜″ to our first setting of 2½″.) With the mat guide set on 2⅞″, mark your mat again using lines that are *only* long enough to bisect the initial 2½″ lines from step 1. This is very important. (See Diagram B.)

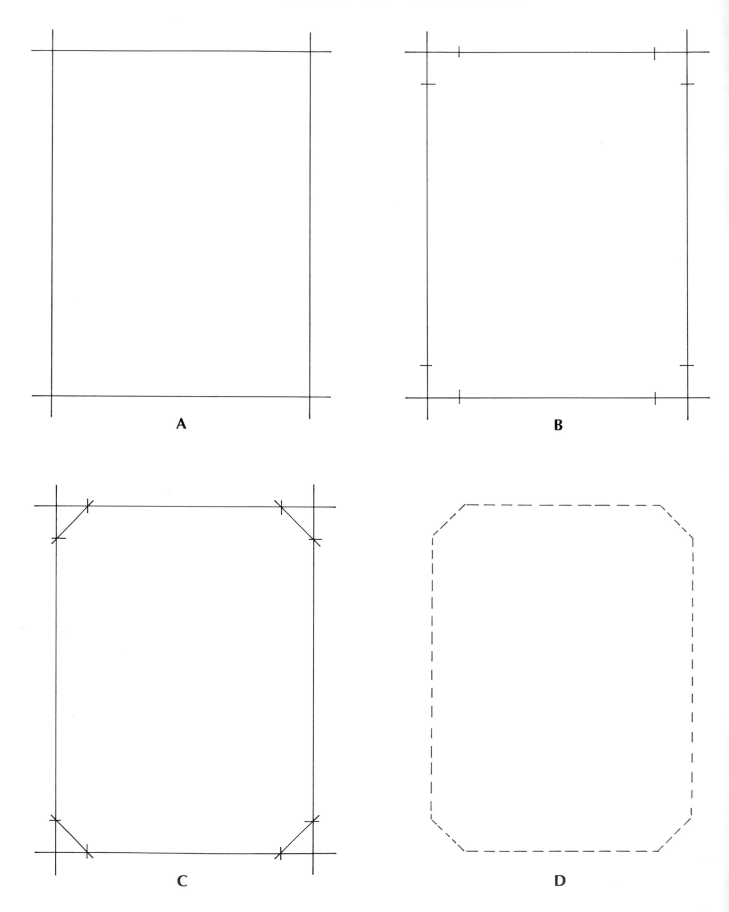

A

B

C

D

3. Using some sort of a straight edge, draw a line that connects the bisecting lines from step 2 in all four corners of the mat. (See Diagram C.)

4. *Take the mat guide off your cutter* and cut out the opening you have created in steps 1–3. (Outline it in red, as shown in Diagram D.)

You should now have a ⅜″ Slant Opening mat at 2½″. While this sounds quite complicated it is not. Three-eighths of an inch is the amount of the slant opening and 2½″ is the location of that slant opening in your mat. After we do a few more practice mats, it should be quite comfortable for you. If you are feeling confused, go back to step 1 and go through it again. Just stick with it and you will get it.

> **NOTE:** It is very important to take the mat guide off the cutter before cutting out the slant corner opening. While you could cut the straight sides with the guide on, you do have to take it off to cut the slants. We feel it is easier to take it off for cutting the whole mat. You should also be aware that when cutting out these slants, you are no longer dealing with a 90 degree angle. Therefore, your undercut and overcut will be a little less than you are normally used to. It should take only a few practice mats for you to make the proper adjustments in your cutting technique.

SLANT CORNER OPENING—PRACTICE MAT TWO

For our second Slant Corner Opening mat, let's do a ½″ slant opening at 2⅜″. I know that may sound like gobbledygook, but we're going to break it down into understandable pieces and quite soon you should be comfortable with this new terminology.

Our first step is to size another piece of matboard to 11″ × 14″. Remembering that our first setting on the guide is always the location in the mat, we will proceed as follows. (We're doing a ½″ slant opening at 2⅜″.)

1. Set your mat guide on 2⅜″ and mark your mat in the usual way.

2. Move your guide to 2⅞″ and draw lines *only* long enough to bisect the lines drawn in step 1. (This second setting was determined by adding the amount of the slant desired—½″—to the location in the board—2⅜″.)

3. Using a ruler, draw the slant lines on your mat. If this confuses you, refer back to the red markings of Diagram D in our first example.

4. Remove the mat guide from your cutter and cut out the slant opening mat you have laid out. Keep in mind that the slant corners are not 90 degree angles and your undercut and overcut allowance will be less than normal.

After completing this second mat, compare it with the first one you cut. Note the visual difference between the two slant openings. Because each slant is perceptibly different in visual effect, it is important for you to make lots of samples. Practice will help you develop the facility you need to produce these mats quickly and profitably. Also, you are going to need lots of corner samples for designing framing of your own inventory and, more importantly, for working with your customers.

SLANT CORNER OPENING—PRACTICE MAT THREE

Let's make one more sample of a Slant Opening mat before we move on. This time it will be a ¼" slant opening at 2¼". Proceed as follows:

1. Size a matboard to 11" × 14".

2. Set your mat guide on 2¼"—the location of the slant opening in the mat. Mark the mat blank in the usual way.

3. Move your mat guide to 2½" and mark lines *only* long enough to bisect the lines drawn in step 2. (We determined this setting by adding the amount of the slant to the location in the mat.)

4. Draw lines that define the slant corners.

5. Remove the mat guide and cut out the opening.

Once again, compare this new mat with practice mats one and two and note the visual differences. Remember that any amount of slant at any location in a mat is possible, so continue to experiment and save your samples for reference and selling tools.

It is very important that you review this section until you are totally comfortable with all the material. Don't try to move on until you're sure

SLANT CORNER OPENINGS

⅜″ Slant Corner Opening at 2½″—
"V-Groove" at 2″

½″ Slant Corner Opening at 2⅜″

2¼″ Border with ¼″ Slant Corner
Opening—"V-Groove" at 1″

of it. The Slant Corner concept is an essential foundation that, once understood, will enable you to create more exotic "V-Grooves" and some really interesting decorative corners.

> **SUGGESTED PRICING:** The charge for a Slant Opening mat is $4.00/mat ($1.00/corner). As always, this is in addition to your charge for the piece of matboard and a "V-Groove" if used.

Notch Cut Corners

The next technique we want to cover with you is the Notch Cut. This corner reminds me of the tabs that were used to hold photographs in albums some years ago, and as such I started out using it in framing my customers' photos. It certainly works beautifully for that, but use your imagination and we are sure you'll find lots of other framing situations where this corner will add that extra touch of design.

The key to accomplishing this corner is remembering that a *Notch Cut always works out of a ¾" Slant Opening*. Therefore every time you want to execute a Notch Cut, you must first create a ¾" Slant Opening in your matboard. With this in mind, after sizing a mat blank, proceed as follows:

1. Using a 3" border, set your mat guide and mark the mat.

2. Since we know we have to create a ¾" Slant Opening first, we do so by adding the amount of the slant to our initial 3" setting. Set the mat guide on 3¾" and make your lines just long enough to bisect the 3" lines from step 1. (See Diagram A on page 78.) (If you are at all confused about this, refer back to the earlier discussion of Slant Corner Opening mats.)

3. Draw lines that define the slant corners. (See Diagram B.)

4. Remove the mat guide and cut out the opening. You should now have a 3" mat with a ¾" slant opening.

5. Put the guide back on the cutter, set it on 3⅛", and mark the same piece of matboard again as shown in Diagram C.

LAYOUT FOR NOTCH CUT CORNERS

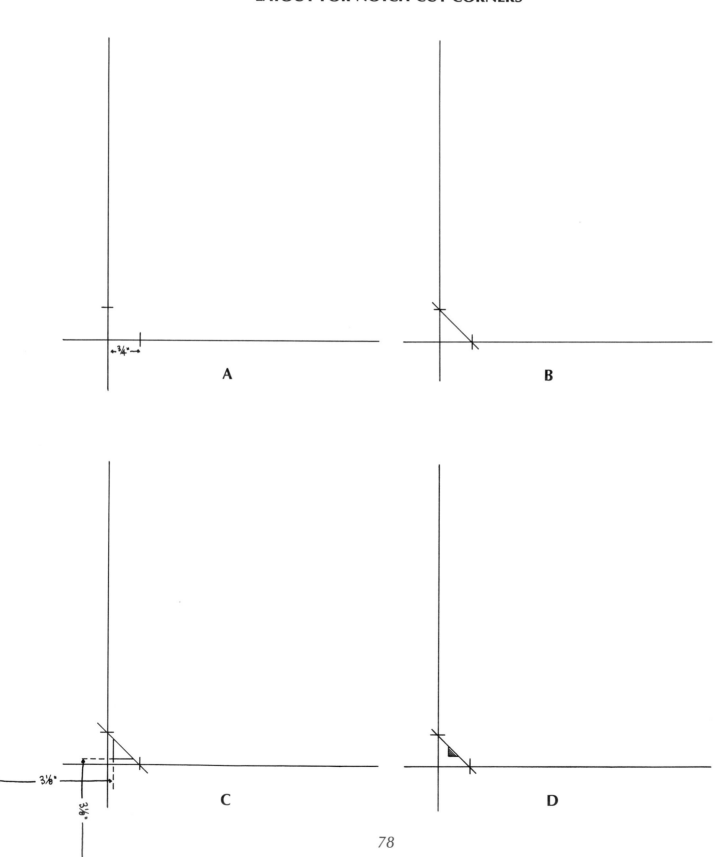

A

B

C

D

NOTCH CUT CORNERS

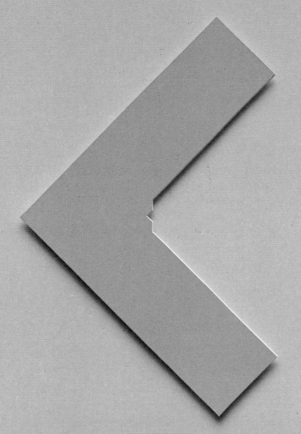

3″ Corner with ¼″ Notch Corner Opening

**3″ Corner with ¼″ Notch Corner
Opening and "V-Groove" at 2″**

**3″ Corner with ⅛″ Notch Corner
Opening and "V-Groove" at 1″**

6. Using the guide set at 3⅛", cut out the shaded area shown in Diagram D on page 78.

We call this a ⅛" Notch Cut as that's the amount added to our initial 3" setting. It really is not difficult if you remember that you must always begin by creating a ¾" slant opening.

Now, in order to get some practice with this corner and so that you can see the visual difference, let's create a ¼" Notch Cut.

¼" NOTCH CUT CORNER WITH "V-GROOVE"— PRACTICE MAT

1. Begin once again by cutting your blank to size. Let's add a little extra design to this one by putting a "V-Groove" in the board at 2". This should be done first, then proceed as before. (If at any point you get confused, refer back to the diagrams we used to illustrate the ⅛" Notch Cut.)

2. Set your mat guide on 3" and mark your mat.

3. Move your guide to 3¾" and again mark the mat.

4. Connect the lines to define the slant opening.

5. Remove your mat guide and cut out the slant opening.

6. Replace the guide on the cutter, set on 3¼", and again mark the same piece of board.

7. Using the guide, cut the small wedge out of each corner that creates the Notch.

Be sure to compare this ¼" Notch with the ⅛" Notch we cut previously. Neither one is better than the other, but it is important that you be aware of their different "feel." Design situations will come up where one may look better than the other, and you must be able to make that decision.

SUGGESTED PRICING: Notch Cut Corners are $4.00/mat. (The same charge as for Slant Corner Openings.)

Double Matting with Notch Cut Corners

Now that you know how to execute a Notch Cut Corner, let's take a look at creating a double mat with that look. <u>This is one of those double mats where you will have to begin by cutting two boards to *exactly* the same size.</u> If you try to accomplish this corner by taping the second board behind the first opening, you are going to get poor results. So size them identically, cut them separately, and then put them together. As long as you are *sure* that the two boards are exactly the same size before you begin, you will not have any problem.

After much experimentation, we have found two different combinations with Double Notch Corner mats that work well. These are as follows:

- *A ⅛" Notch Corner mat for the outer mat and a ¼" Notch Corner mat for the inner cuff.* This looks good with whatever width of outer mat you want to use (as long as it is not too narrow) and either a ⅛" or ¼" cuff. A reasonable guideline for the width of the outer mat would be 2" or larger.

- *A ¼" Notch Corner mat for the outer mat and a ⅛" Notch Corner mat for the inner cuff.* This is just the reverse of the mat described above.

You must not let the execution of this double mat confuse you. Cut the outer mat by following the step-by-step instructions we gave you on pages 77–80. For your inner mat, proceed by the following steps.

1. After deciding on the width of the cuff (or inner mat) that you would like, set your mat guide by adding that amount to the width of your

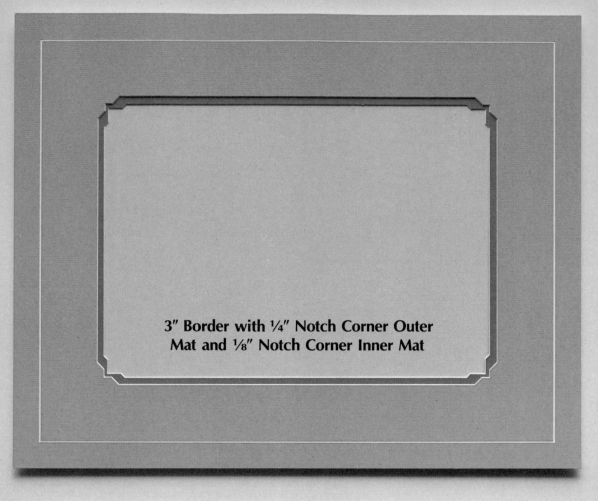

3″ Border with ¼″ Notch Corner Outer Mat and ⅛″ Notch Corner Inner Mat

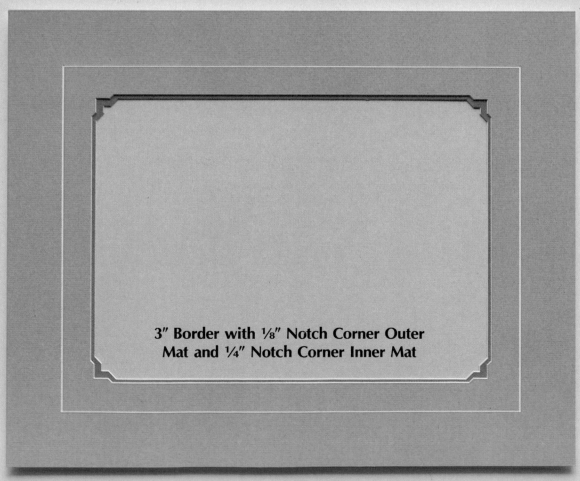

3″ Border with ⅛″ Notch Corner Outer Mat and ¼″ Notch Corner Inner Mat

outer mat. (If your outer mat width is 3″ and you want a ⅛″ cuff, add ⅛″ to 3″ and set your guide on 3⅛″.)

2. Remembering that Notch Cut Corners always work out of a ¾″ slant opening, add the ¾″ to your first setting of 3⅛″. Your guide should now be set on 3⅞″.

3. Using your mat guide, draw lines only long enough to bisect the 3⅛″ lines from step 1. Use a straight edge of some kind to draw in the lines that define your slant corner opening.

4. Remove the mat guide from the cutter and cut out the slant corner opening you have just laid out.

5. Put the mat guide back onto your cutter and set it on 3⅜″. (Since our inner mat is going to be a ¼″ Notch Cut Corner, you add that amount to our initial setting of 3⅛″.) Using the guide, mark your mat and cut it.

6. Take the two pieces of matboard you have cut, align the outer edges all around, and tape them together using Scotch ATG.

As always, we think this mat looks even better with a "V-Groove" and in the future that should be done first.

Just to get some more practice and to have another selling tool, go ahead and cut another Double Notch Cut Corner mat. This time make the outer mat a ¼″ Notch Cut, the inner mat a ⅛″, and begin by putting a "V-Groove" in the outer mat.

We have done a great deal of experimenting with this cut and feel that the two double mat combinations we have given you are the most practical for regular use. However, we always encourage you to do some experimenting on your own. We are sure that you will come up with some great looking new combinations.

> **SUGGESTED PRICING:** Notch Cut Corner double mats should be $4.00/mat *plus* your regular charge for each of the matboards. The charge for including the recommended "V-Groove" in this mat would be an additional .15/united inch.

The Slant Corner "V-Groove"

Moving along, the next logical step for our progression through the world of "Creative Mat Designing" is to take our knowledge of the Slant Corner Concept and apply it to executing a Slant Corner "V-Groove." It is really quite simple, and you have probably already figured it out on your own. But just to be certain you understand it completely, let's do it step by step.

1. Begin by reviewing the instructions for creating a Slant Corner Opening mat which are found on pages 71–73, as steps 1–4 will be identical. *Note:* In step 1, put a reference mark on the back of the mat while marking it. This is going to be a Slant Corner *"V-Groove,"* rather than a Slant Corner Opening, so we will need to be able to put the center back exactly as it comes out. Since we are going to duplicate the dimensions for the mat that we did on pages 71–73, it will become a ⅜" Slant "V-Groove" at 2½". Please don't let this terminology throw you; it will become quite clear as we go along.

5. Move your guide over until it contacts the "V-Groove" stop on your mat cutter and tighten it. (There is no change in the setting of that "V-Groove" stop. Once it is adjusted for the width we prefer, we always leave it the same.)

6. Place the center (or dropout) of your mat back into the cutter FACE UP and remove the strips from all sides. This center will have slant corners, so you will be making eight cuts instead of four.

    You will want to make sure that those slants are squarely against your guide when you cut. Be sure to cut slowly and smoothly and treat them gently. (This might be a good place to refer back to the section on cutting technique.)

SLANT CORNER "V-GROOVES"

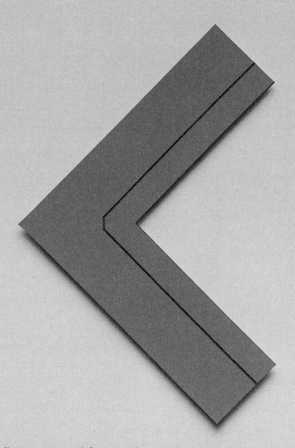

3″ Corner with ¼″ Slant "V-Groove" at 2″

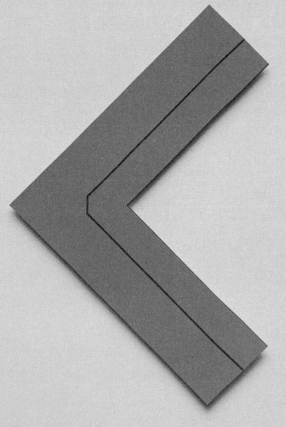

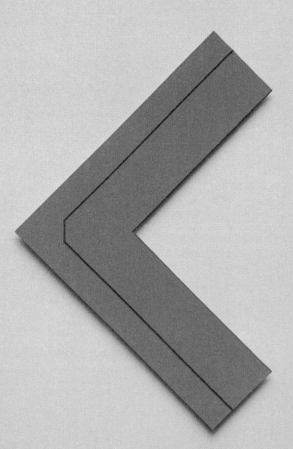

3″ Corner with ⅜″ Slant "V-Groove" at 1¾″

3″ Corner with ½″ Slant "V-Groove" at 1″

7. Place the altered center FACE DOWN and place your mat over it while lining up the reference marks. Tape the two pieces together with Scotch 810 tape. We always tape the four slant corners first and then put long strips along the straight sides of the mat. This provides some extra reenforcement for the slant corners of the "V-Groove."

    Turn your mat right side up and examine your Slant "V-Groove" to make sure the corners have lined up correctly. If they have not, you'll have to untape the center and realign. If you align your reference marks carefully the first time, you should not have any problems.

8. Set your mat guide on 3", or whatever width you want for a border, mark the mat, and cut out your opening.

You can easily see that this Slant Corner "V-Groove" has a different look than the regular groove you learned earlier. This is an important addition to your growing repertoire.

As far as designing with the Slant Corner "V-Groove," we feel that it can be used any place you might use a regular "V-Groove." The choice is up to you or to you and your customer. We feel that the more traditional the artwork, the more likely that a regular "V-Groove" would be preferable. But, there is never any one solution and it is often a matter of personal taste. Make samples that include both kinds of grooves and offer the choice to your customer.

Just to give you some more practice on Slant Corner "V-Grooves," we suggest you execute the following mats. For each of them use a 3" border.

- A ¼" Slant "V-Groove" at 2"

- A ⅜" Slant "V-Groove" at 1¾"

- A ½" Slant "V-Groove" at 1"

When you have finished, compare all the samples that you have made, noting the visual differences between them. These are but a few of the possibilities with Slant Corner "V-Grooves," so be sure to do some exploring on your own.

SUGGESTED PRICING: The recommended charge for a Slant Corner "V-Groove" is .20/united inch.

TROUBLESHOOTING THE SLANT CORNER "V-GROOVE"

As the matting we discuss becomes more sophisticated, it becomes increasingly important for you to use the correct technique when executing. If you don't, you will find that the finished mats are going to be lacking that real "quality" look and that customers just will not be willing to pay for them. Unfortunately, with the techniques that we are covering, any mistakes will really stick out in a mat. It is crucial for you to take the time to practice as much as is necessary to get perfect results.

Below are some problems and solutions relating to Slant Corner "V-Grooves."

- *The slant corners on your mat and your center are not parallel when you tape them back together.* Be extra careful that the slant corner is absolutely flush against the guide for its entire length when you trim it face up.

- *The slant corners on your "V-Grooved" center are curved or hooked.* Don't "take a run" at that center when you are trimming it. Lower your blade right at the upper edge of the board and move through it slowly and smoothly. If the problem persists, make sure you have removed your slip sheet when trimming the center. This is essential when doing a "V-Groove" of any kind.

If you pay attention to all of these details, your Slant Corner "V-Grooves" should come out perfectly every time. These little tricks will soon become second nature for you; just remember to *keep practicing.*

SLANT CORNER "V-GROOVE" WITH SLANT CORNER OPENING: "A FRAME WITHIN A FRAME"

You have probably already anticipated the next step in our progression into "Creative Matting," as it is quite logical. For the first time you will be able to see how combining two relatively simple techniques can result in eye-catching mat design.

If you are totally comfortable with the methods for creating a Slant Corner Opening as well as the Slant Corner "V-Groove," you should review those sections before proceeding.

Our goal is to create one of each of the above in the same mat, and if you know how to do each separately, the combination shouldn't give you any trouble. Remember to work from the outside of the mat toward the center: this means we will be executing our Slant Corner "V-Groove" first. With this in mind, put a ¼" Slant Corner "V-Groove" in a piece of matboard at 2". Next, in the same piece of board, cut a ¼" Slant Opening at 3". The first thing you should notice is the way the Slant Opening echoes the Slant Corner "V-Groove" and creates a "frame" within a frame." Trust us, this is one that your customers will rave over.

Please continue by executing the following mats:

- A 3" mat with a ⅜" Slant "V-Groove" at 1⅞" and a ⅜" Slant Corner Opening at 3".

- A 3" mat with a ½" Slant "V-Groove" at 1" and a ½" Slant Corner Opening at 3".

- A 3" mat with a ¼" Slant "V-Groove" at 2" and a ½" Slant Corner Opening at 3".

Take a good look at these and catalog the visual differences in your mind. In particular, note the "look" that is achieved when the slant on the opening is not the same as that on the "V-Groove" (as in the last mat listed above). By now you should have many samples to show your customers and a variety of techniques to work with when designing. There is never any one solution for a framing job, so use your imagination and creativity to come up with mats that will really set your framing apart from that of the other shops your existing or potential clients might visit.

SUGGESTED PRICING: The regular charge for whatever type of matboard you use *plus* .20/united inch for the Slant Corner "V-Groove" *plus* $4.00 for the Slant Corner Opening.

As the charges begin to add up, you can see that it really is worth the time and effort to sell more "creative" matting. It's not only the increased revenues that make it important, but the very real reward of growing customer satisfaction and appreciation.

PLACEMENT OF SLANT CORNER "V-GROOVES" WITH SLANT CORNER OPENINGS

3" Corner with ⅜" Slant "V-Groove" at
1⅞" and ⅜" Slant Corner Opening

3" Corner with ½" Slant "V-Groove" at 1"
and ½" Slant Corner Opening

3" Corner with ¼" Slant "V-Groove" at 2"
and ½" Slant Corner Opening

Authors' Thoughts on the Use of "V-Grooves"

Now that you know how to execute both Regular and Slant Corner "V-Grooves," we want to emphasize again how important we feel they are. There is no other single technique that we discuss in this text that can do as much to add style and design to your matting. With this fact in mind, you should assume that all the mats you design from here on will include a "V-Groove" of some kind, be it Regular or Slant Cornered. The decision of what kind to use and where it should be placed in the mat is left to you and your customer. Of course, should the client request specifically not to have a groove, you would have to comply with that request. In the ten years since we began working with the groove, we have included it in almost every frame we've designed for the gallery or for a customer. No one has ever asked to take it out of a mat or said they didn't like the way it looks. It will probably happen one of these days, but so far so good. You must not underestimate the reaction you are going to get from your customers when you start designing with "V-Grooves." It is the single best design trick that we know, and it will bring you substantial new profits on your matting work. Get some up on display in your gallery or frameshop and they will sell themselves.

Multiple "V-Grooves"

Once you are comfortable with the design and execution of a "V-Groove," the next logical step is to use more than one groove in the same mat. This can be a very effective technique. It provides a look that resembles a three-dimensional French mat. In addition to the visual effects, you also add extra value to a mat. (Each "V-Groove" will be charged for separately per united inch.)

The possible combinations of grooves and their locations in a mat are almost endless. We are going to give you some suggestions and show photographs of those that we have found to be effective in our designs. As always, we encourage you to do plenty of experimenting on your own. There just isn't any one "best" combination, and you will want to have as many as possible in your "bag of tricks."

TWO REGULAR "V-GROOVES" ¼" APART

Following are some suggested combinations for "V-Grooves" ¼" apart.

- In a 2½" mat, at 1¾" and at 2"

- In a 2½" mat, at 1" and 1¼"

- In a 3" mat, at 2" and 2¼"

- In a 3" mat, at 2¼" and 2½"

- In a 3" mat, at 1" and 1¼"

MULTIPLE GROOVES: ¼″ APART

2½″ Corner—"V-Grooves" at
1¾″ and 2″

3″ Corner—"V-Grooves" at 2″
and 2¼″

2½″ Corner—"V-Grooves" at
1″ and 1¼″

3″ Corner—"V-Grooves" at
2¼″ and 2½″

3″ Corner—"V-Grooves" at 1″
and ¼″

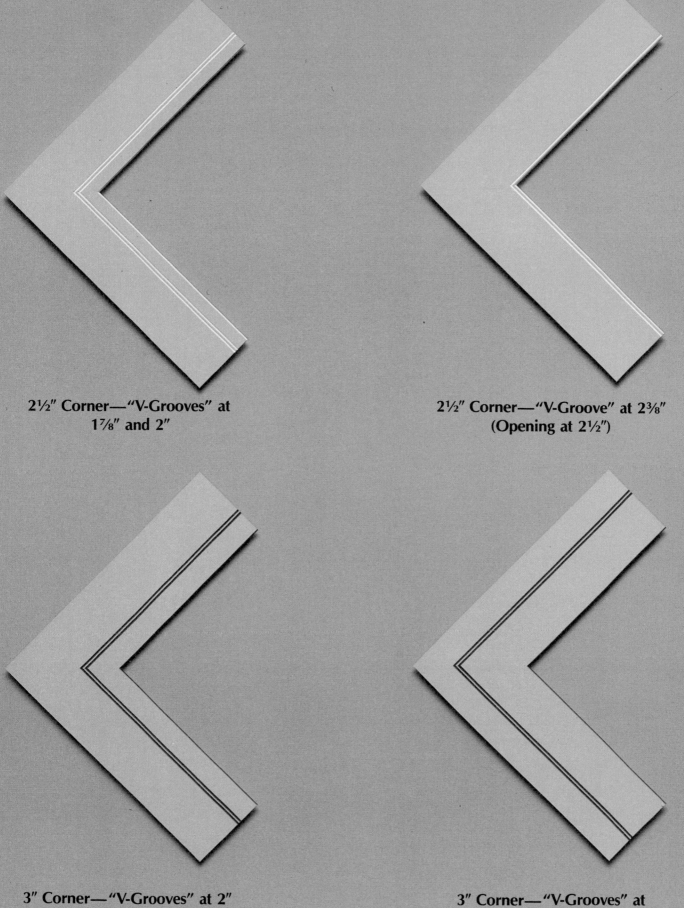

2½″ Corner—"V-Grooves" at
1⅞″ and 2″

2½″ Corner—"V-Groove" at 2⅜″
(Opening at 2½″)

3″ Corner—"V-Grooves" at 2″
and 2⅛″

3″ Corner—"V-Grooves" at
1⅛″ and 1¼″

We are not saying that grooves ¼" apart can be used only in 2½" or 3" mats, but we do feel that it would look pretty busy if your mat border becomes too narrow. You might keep that in mind when designing.

SUGGESTED PRICING: .15/united inch per groove.

TWO REGULAR "V-GROOVES" ⅛" APART

Before giving you formulas for this particular pattern, we want to give you a tip for executing it. With the grooves only ⅛" apart, it can be tricky to cut. We get the best results when we cut the groove nearest the opening first and then move toward the outside and cut the second groove. In addition, it is a good idea to purposely undercut these and then use a good sharp blade to release the corner. (A single- or double-edge razor blade works best for this.) It may take some practice for you to execute this one perfectly, but the results will be worth your effort.

- In a 2½" mat at 1⅞" and 2"

- In a 2½" mat at ⅞" and 1"

- In a 2½" mat at 2⅜" (In this mat the second groove is not a groove, but your opening.)

- In a 3" mat at 2" and 2⅛"

- In a 3" mat at 2⅜" and 2½"

- In a 3" mat at 1⅛" and 1¼"

SUGGESTED PRICING: .15/united inch per groove.

ONE REGULAR GROOVE AND ONE SLANT GROOVE ¼" APART

- In a 3" mat at 1¾" and 2"

- In a 3" mat at 1" and 1¼"

94

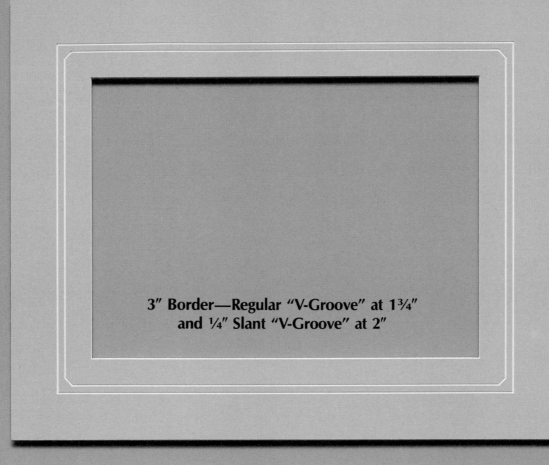

**3″ Border—Regular "V-Groove" at 1¾″
and ¼″ Slant "V-Groove" at 2″**

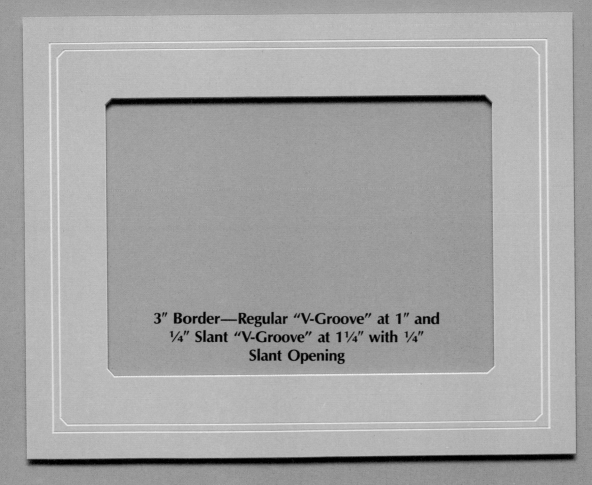

**3″ Border—Regular "V-Groove" at 1″ and
¼″ Slant "V-Groove" at 1¼″ with ¼″
Slant Opening**

We really feel that this particular pattern is too much for a 2½" mat. However, you should make your own decision about that. As we mentioned at the beginning of this section, there is a tremendous amount of flexibility in the placement of multiple grooves in your mats, with the final decision of what looks good depending on individual taste.

SUGGESTED PRICING: .15/united inch for the Regular "V-Groove" *plus* .20/united inch for the Slant Corner "V-Groove." For ease in figuring pricing, we suggest you add the two united inch charges together and multiply by the number of united inches to determine your charge.

The Double Track "V-Groove"

While this cut also involves a pair of "V-Grooves," we have given it a specific name and want to treat it as a separate entity.

There are a couple of things you should know about this particular design. First, *it looks best in a 3" mat or larger*. It is just too busy visually to be used in anything smaller. Second, *it looks best nearer the frame rather than the opening of the mat*. Keep those two items in mind and proceed as follows:

1. Assuming a 3" border, set your guide on 1¼" and put a Regular "V-Groove" in the board at that setting. When you finish cutting, be particularly careful to tape the pieces back together securely.

2. In the same piece of matboard, put a 1" Slant Corner "V-Groove" at 1". (Since 1" is the location, that is the first setting on your guide.) After marking your mat blank there, move your guide to 2" (you are adding the amount of the slant to your first setting of 1", and make lines that are only long enough to bisect the 1" lines.

3. Go ahead and cut out the Slant Corner mat you have marked and then "V-Groove" the center. When you do this, you will be cutting across the Regular "V-Groove" that you cut in step 1. While you can feel it, it will not be a problem as the Scotch 810 tape is quite thin. Again, when you finish cutting, tape it back together securely.

4. Set your guide on 3" and cut out your opening.

Because my gallery is located in Vermont near several large ski resorts, I initially developed this pattern of "V-Grooves" to use on prints

**3" Border with a Double Track
"V-Groove" and ¼" Slant Opening**

**3" Border with a Double Track
"V-Groove" and Regular Opening**

depicting skiing. It reminded me of the tracks in the snow that a skier might make. Later on, I began using it on prints and posters that involved boats and sailing as it brought to mind the rigging. Both applications have been well received by my customers. I am sure you will find even more subjects on which it is attractive.

Just for practice, execute a second Double Track "V-Groove" in another piece of board and this time give it a ¼" Slant Corner Opening. This will give you another sample to use in your designing and a chance to see a different effect.

SUGGESTED PRICING: .15/united inch for the Regular "V-Groove" *plus* .20/united inch for the Slant Corner "V-Groove" or a combined united inch charge of .35/united inch. If a Slant Corner Opening is used, the charge would be an additional $4.00 ($1.00/corner).

The Deco Corner

After so much talk about "V-Grooves," it is time for us to move on and add decorative corner cuts to our list of creative mat techniques. The first one of these we will teach you is called a Deco Corner. It's very easy to execute, as you will soon see, and it really adds a feeling of "design" to a mat.

1. Cut a piece of matboard to a size 16″ × 20″ or larger.

2. Assuming a 3″ border for our mat, set the mat guide on 3″ and mark the blank.

3. Move the mat guide to 3⅝″ and mark your mat again. Make these lines long enough to define a square in each of the four corners of the mat blank. (See Diagram A.)

4. Move the mat guide to 4″ and mark the blank for the third time. These lines should be *only* long enough to bisect the 3″ lines we drew in step 2 above. (See Diagram B.)

5. Cut out the small squares created in the four corners of the mat by steps 2 and 3. (See shaded area of Diagram C.) It will be necessary to remove your mat guide from the cutter to complete this step. <u>Be careful to avoid any reverse bevels.</u>

6. Cut out the 1″ slant opening at 3″ which you laid out in step 4. (See the dotted red line in Diagram D that defines the slant corner.)

Just as with previous mats, if you want to use a "V-Groove" with this decorative corner it should be executed first. As we are sure you know by now, our feeling is that a "V-Groove" adds design and value to every mat, so you should make samples of Deco Corners that include them.

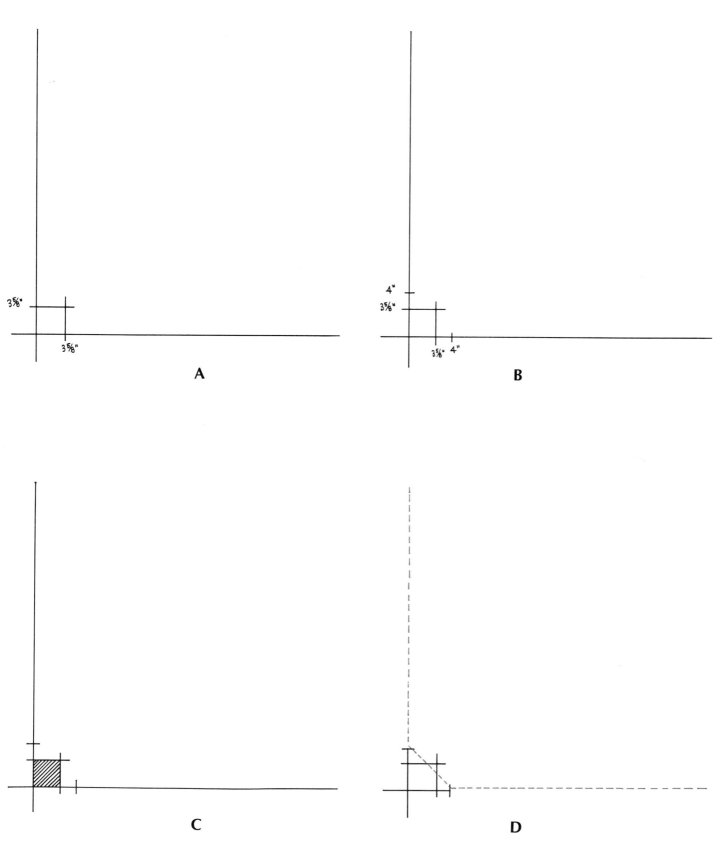

3⅝"

A

4"
3⅝"

3⅝" 4"

B

C

D

DECO CORNER

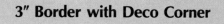

3″ Border with Deco Corner

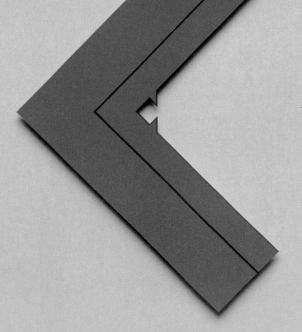

3″ Border with Deco Corner—Regular
"V-Groove" at 2″

3″ Border with Deco Corner—⅜″ slan
"V-Groove" at 1″

DOUBLE MAT WITH DECO CORNER

**3″ Border with ¼″ Slant "V-Groove" at 2″
Deco Corner Opening with ⅛″ Inner Mat**

SUGGESTED PRICING: Deco Corners are $10.00/mat ($2.50/corner). This charge is in addition to the normal united inch charge for the board that you are using *plus* the united inch charge for a "V-Groove" if used.

A DOUBLE MAT WITH THE DECO CORNER

Adding a double mat to a Deco Corner can be accomplished with the following very simple steps. (See photo on page 103.)

1. Select the color of matting that you wish to use for your inner cuff and cut it to *exactly the same size* as your outer mat. This is absolutely essential to insure that your two mats will line up perfectly.

2. Add the width of the inner mat that you would like to have to whatever the width your outer mat is and set your mat guide on that figure. (We used a 3" border for our sample and we will make our inner cuff ⅛", so the mat guide would be set on 3⅛".) While the width of the inner mat is a matter of personal taste, we have found that most of the time with this particular corner a ⅛" cuff looks best.

3. With your mat guide set on 3⅛", mark and cut out your mat. Treat this just as if it were a basic single mat.

4. Put ATG tape on the back of your outer mat on all four sides next to the opening and stick the two mats together. Be certain that the outside edges of the two pieces line up precisely.

If the outer dimensions of your two mat blanks were indeed identical, you should have a great looking double mat with a Deco Corner. If for some reason the two pieces did not line up perfectly, you will want to take a little more care when sizing the blanks for your next attempt.

SUGGESTED PRICING: The regular united inch charge for a double mat *plus* $10.00 for the Deco Corners in the outer mat. If you include a "V-Groove," and we recommend that you do, add the appropriate united inch charge for the type you use.

The Baronial Corner

The next decorative corner we are going to teach you is called the Baronial. While it does take a little time to get comfortable with the layout of this one, it is well worth the effort as there are two additional decorative corners that will derive from the exact same markings. Let's go through the Baronial first and then move on from there.

1. Cut a board to 16″ × 20″ or larger.

2. Assuming a 3″ border width, set your guide on 3″ and mark your mat.

3. Move your guide to 3½″ and again mark the blank. These lines should be only long enough to intersect the 3″ lines you drew in step 2 above.

4. Move your guide to 4″ and mark the points where that setting intersects the 3″ lines. Once again, these lines should be drawn sparingly. (See Diagram A on page 106.)

5. Draw a diagonal line that connects the two 3½″ lines from step 3. Do the same thing with the 4″ lines drawn in step 4. (See Diagram B.)

6. Measure and mark ⁹⁄₁₆″ from the points where the 4″ diagonal line intersects with the 3″ lines. Connect those two ⁹⁄₁₆″ points to the points where the 3½″ diagonal line intersects with the 3″ lines. Extend these new lines in toward the center of your mat until they cross. (See Diagram C.)

7. Remove the mat guide from your cutter and cut out the small triangle that you have created in all four corners of your mat. (See shaded area of Diagram D.) *As always, be careful to avoid reverse bevels.*

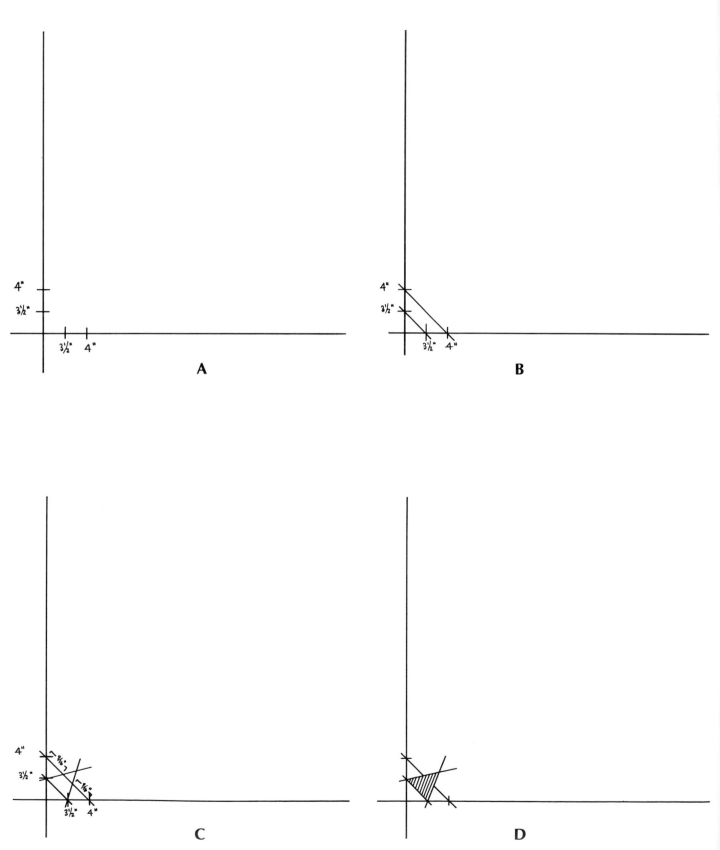

A

B

C

D

BARONIAL CORNER

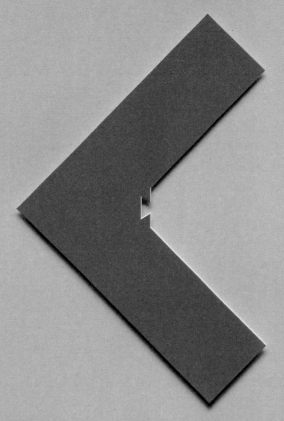

3″ Border with Baronial Corner

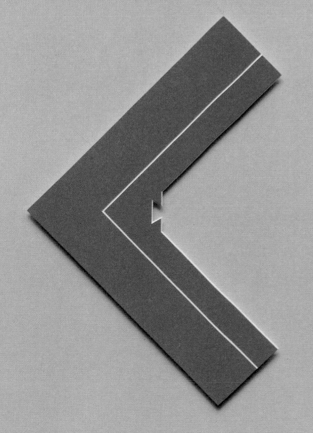

**3″ Border with Baronial Corner—Regular
"V-Groove" at 2″**

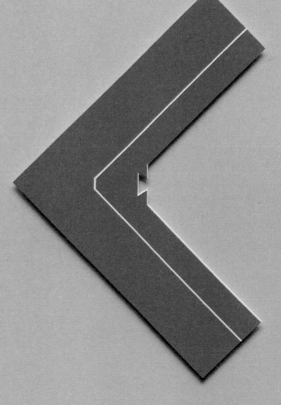

**3″ Border with Baronial Corner—¼″
Slant "V-Groove" at 2″**

8. Complete your mat by cutting out the 1″ slant opening at 3″ which you have already laid out.

This corner, like the others we've discussed, would look still better with the addition of a "V-Groove." In order for you to be more comfortable with the layout of this particular cut, at this point we would like you to execute two more samples and include a "V-Groove" in each: one Regular, and one Slant Corner. You might also refer to the photograph of our prize-winning entry in the 1983 PPFA New and Creative Framing Competition which incorporates the Baronial Corner in the mat design. (See page v.)

We do have one further design tip for you on this particular corner. Because it is visually quite busy, we have found that the Baronial Corner is best used as a single mat. It does, however, look especially nice with a Window Mount, and you really should make a sample of this treatment to show your customers. The above comments do not apply to the use of a "V-Groove." We're sure you understand by now that we feel a "V-Groove" adds valid design to every mat.

SUGGESTED PRICING: Baronial Corners are $10.00/mat ($2.50/corner). This is in addition to regular charges for the matboard and a "V-Groove" if used.

The Decoronial Corner

As we mentioned when we began the discussion on Baronial Corners, there are actually three different decorative cuts that begin with the exact same marking of the mat blank. After the Baronial, the second is called the Decoronial. You are probably beginning to think that some of the names we've given our techniques are absurd, but we had to call them something. And in fact, the Decoronial is a combination of the Deco and the Baronial Corners.

1. Our first 6 steps will be the same as those taken for laying out the Baronial Corner. This would be a good place for you to review those steps. We have repeated Diagrams A, B, and C here for your reference. (See page 110.) Please note that with this corner you may eliminate the line connecting the two 3½" lines in Diagram B.

7. The only difference between this corner and the Baronial is that instead of cutting out a triangle as we did before, we are going to cut out a kite shape. (See shaded area of Diagram D.) You will need to remove your mat guide to accomplish this and again, *be careful to avoid reverse bevels*.

8. Complete the mat by cutting out the 1" slant opening at 3" which you have already laid out.

Compare the Baronial Corner mat that you did earlier with the Decoronial Corner mat which you have just completed. Remember that neither one is better than the other, but rather two separate design options that you now have to offer your clients.

109

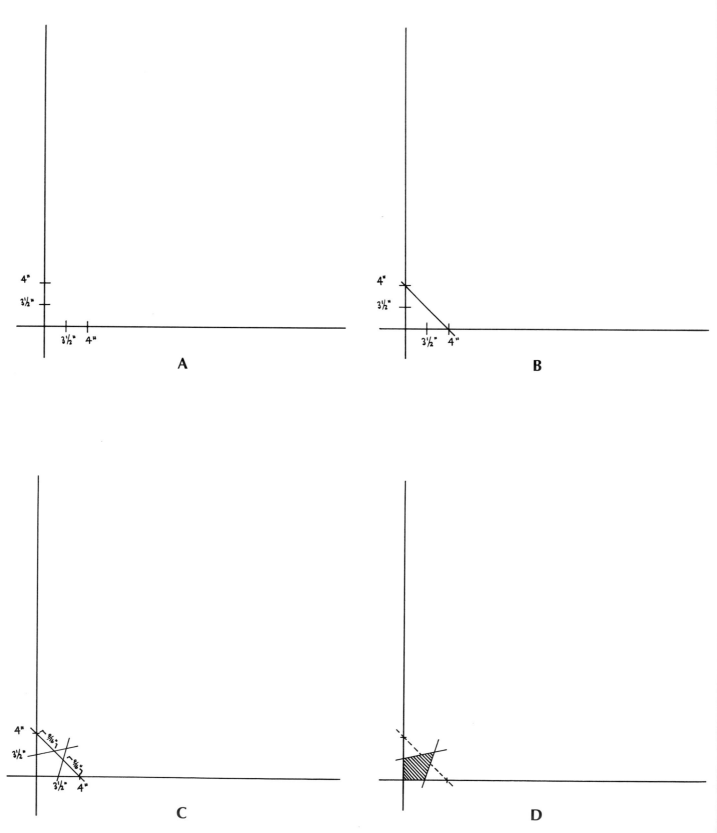

DECORONIAL CORNER

3″ Border with Decoronial Corner

**3″ Border with Decoronial Corner—
Regular "V-Groove" at 2″**

**3″ Border with Decoronial Corner—³⁄₈″
Slant "V-Groove" at 1″**

**3″ Border with Decoronial Corner—
Regular "V-Groove" at 2″ and ¹⁄₈″ Inner Mat**

Just to get a little more practice in laying out and executing the Decoronial Corner, go ahead and make two more samples and this time incorporate a Regular "V-Groove" in one and a Slant Corner "V-Groove" in the other.

> **SUGGESTED PRICING:** The Decoronial Corner is $10.00/mat ($2.50/corner). As always, the charge for the matboard and the type of "V-Groove" used would be additional.

The Cutoff Decoronial Corner

This is the third and last decorative corner derived from the same basic layout that you learned with the Baronial Corner. While the only additional step required is a very minor one, the visual effect of the finished mat is quite different from either of the two preceding cuts. We feel the corner can really stand on its own as a design tool.

1. Follow steps 1–8 of your instructions for executing the Decoronial Corner and then complete the following step.

9. Put your mat guide back on the cutter and set it on 3¼". At that setting cut the tips off the four Decoronial Corners that you have created. Remember to cut from the back of the mat. (See Diagram.)

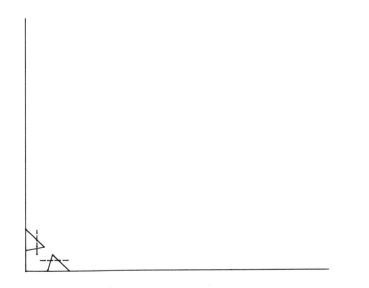

CUTOFF DECORONIAL CORNER

**3″ Border with a Cutoff Decoronial
Corner—½″ Slant "V-Groove" at 1″ and
⅛″ Inner Mat**

> **SUGGESTED PRICING:** The Cutoff Decoronial Corner is also $10.00/mat *plus* charges for the matboard used and a "V-Groove." (Slicing the tips off the basic Decoronial Corner does not take enough time to warrant an additional charge.)

This corner will work very nicely as a double mat (see opposite), and it is executed exactly the same way that you did the double mat with the Deco Corner. If you're interested, refer to page 104.

You will certainly want to compare this new sample with the two you made previously. Although all three corners derive from the same basic layout, they each have their own distinctive look. If you make the effort to design and display some framing that incorporates these new techniques, you should quickly discover that they sell themselves. This is the kind of matting design that will excite your customers, help you merchandise your art and poster inventory, and, at the same time, sell more "creative" framing.

The Keystone Corner

This is one of our favorite corners. It never fails to attract attention when we display it on artwork in the gallery. Although it is one of our most difficult designs to execute, once you have mastered it, the creative and financial rewards make all the learning effort worthwhile.

For our first sample, size your matboard to 11″ × 14″ and then follow the steps below.

1. Planning for a 3″ border, set your mat guide on 1¾″ and mark the mat blank. These lines should intersect in all four corners and extend outward no more than a couple of inches. (See Diagram A.) As we proceed with this mat, you are going to end up with quite a lot of lines on the back of it. Limiting the length of these initial markings will help you keep everything straight.

2. Move the guide to 2¼″ and mark again. These new lines will create a ½″ square in each corner of the board and should be made only long enough to define that square. (See Diagram B.)

3. In order to create a reference mark for each of the squares, number them as shown in Diagram C. After the numbering is complete, remove the guide from your cutter and cut them out. Be particularly careful to avoid getting any reverse bevels and **do not lose track of these four squares**.

    If you have a problem with getting reverse bevels when you don't want them, here is a tip for you. *In cutting, if you always keep the piece of the mat that you want to fall out under the cutting bar, you will never get a reverse bevel.*

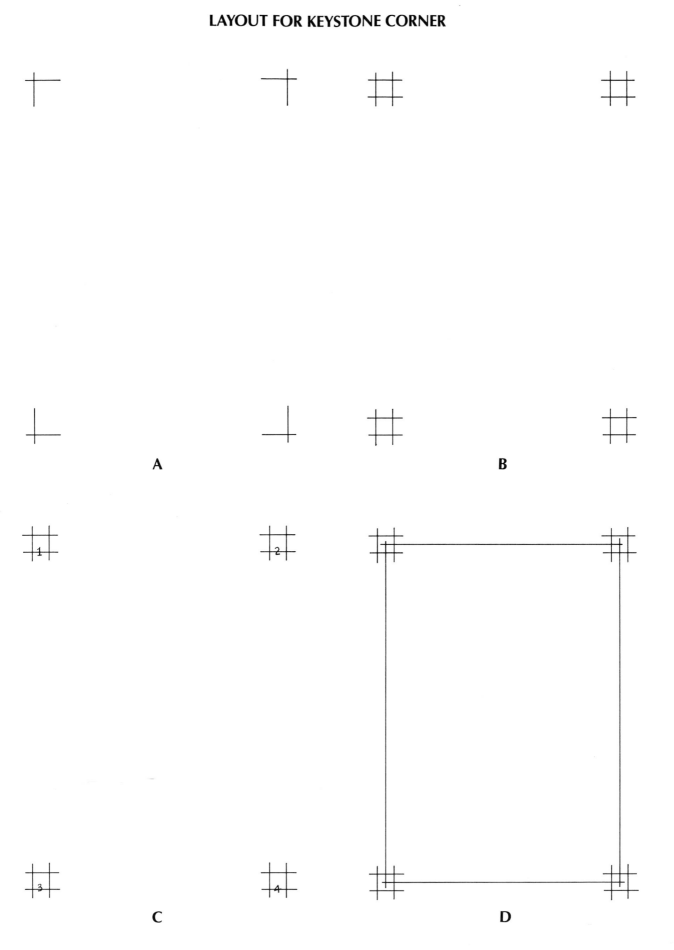

A

B

C

D

4. Take each of the four small squares and "V-Groove" them. *Due to their small size, you will get better results by leaving your slip sheet in the cutter* but, most importantly, you must be sure to move that slip sheet after every single cut to insure working into a fresh surface. This is an exception to the normal rule of removing the slip sheet while "V-Grooving."

5. Using the numbers you made as references, tape the squares back into their proper corners. To be sure that they stay, we suggest you use two overlapping pieces of 810 for each one.

6. Set the guide to 2", mark the mat, and cut out the opening. (You are going to be cutting into the middle of the four squares that you just finished "V-Grooving," but don't let it throw you. You will feel the 810 tape when you get into the corners, but it is thin enough that it won't keep your blade from tracking properly or affect the appearance of the finished mat.) "V-Groove" that dropout piece and tape it back. (See Diagram D on page 117.)

7. Finish this mat by moving the mat guide to 3" and cutting out the opening.

SUGGESTED PRICING: Keystone Corners are $20.00/mat *plus* .15/united inch for the "V-Groove" and the normal charge for the type of board used. When computing the number of united inches for charging purposes, use the outside dimensions of the mat.

As you can see, this mat really has that stylish look that we have been talking about throughout this text. However, with this particular design, any errors in the execution will be extremely obvious and really detract from the overall effect.

In the beginning of this section we mentioned that this is one of our hardest mats to cut cleanly. Here are a few tips that might make your life a little easier.

*   You must use a slip sheet when "V-Grooving" the four small squares. Remember to move it after *each cut* so that you are always working into a fresh surface.

KEYSTONE CORNER MAT

- Cut slowly and smoothly when doing the actual "V-Grooving" and be sure that you are using adequate pressure on the cutter handle directly opposite the piece you are working on. *Adequate* means enough to insure that the piece will not slip while you are cutting, but not *excessive*.

- If you are still having problems after trying the above, execute a couple of Keystone Corner mats with squares that are larger than ½". Obviously, the bigger the squares, the easier they will be to "V-Groove". Once you have polished your technique, you should have no further headaches with the smaller pieces.

- There will be some design situations where you will want to use larger squares for aesthetic reasons. We strongly recommend that everyone prepare for those by making some samples. It will provide valuable practice in "V-Grooving" and prepare you for more difficult small pieces of matboard. And, as you have learned by now, you cannot have too many samples.

A VARIATION ON THE KEYSTONE CORNER

Here is a second version of our Keystone Corner, and it is actually easier to accomplish than the first. We sometimes refer to it as the "Cheater" Keystone. Nonetheless, it has excellent design and will be important as an option to offer your customers.

Just as we did with the Basic Keystone, let's begin by cutting a piece of matboard to 11" × 14". Then follow the steps below.

1. Using a 3" border, set your mat guide on 1¾" and mark your mat blank. Again, these lines should intersect in all four corners and extend outward no more than a couple of inches. (See Diagram A on page 117.)

2. Move the guide to 2¼" and mark again. These new lines will create a ½" square in each corner of the board and should be made only long enough to define that square. (See Diagram B on page 117.)

3. There is no need to number these squares for later reference. After we cut them out they will be discarded. (See, we told you this version was easier.)

KEYSTONE CORNER VARIATION

4. Go ahead and cut out the four squares. Do be careful to avoid getting any reverse bevels.

5. Move your mat guide to 2", mark, and cut out that opening. You will be cutting into the middle of the square holes in each corner of the mat. "V-Groove" that dropout and then tape it back into the mat. *Caution:* You don't want any 810 tape to extend into the square openings.

6. Set your mat guide to 3", mark, and cut out the final opening.

7. Complete this mat by taking a small piece of another color of matboard and removing the facing paper from it. (Just slip a razor blade between the paper and the core of the board and peel it back.) Cut four pieces of that facing paper and tape them behind the square openings in your mat with ATG.

You will immediately notice the different effect you get from this mat. The facing paper that was taped into the square openings provides an accent of color that is quite dramatic. It is particularly eye-catching when it is cut in a Black Core matboard.

And if you want to add still more pizazz, go ahead and make this a double mat with the inner mat color the same as the one used behind the four squares.

> **SUGGESTED PRICING:** The "Cheater" Keystone is $20.00/mat. (Remember, you are charging for your "creativity" rather than just time and materials.) *Plus* .15/united inch for the "V-Groove" and the appropriate charge for the type of matboard used. If you do add that double mat, don't forget to charge for it, too.

4

CIRCLES, OVALS, AND COMBINATION CUTS

Although many framers have explored the creative possibilities of the straight line mat cutter, for some time we have felt that comparatively little has been done with the circle/oval machine and, more particularly, with cuts combining the two. That is exactly what we would like to cover with you in this section of the book.

If you do not have a circle/oval mat cutter, please do not immediately assume that these pages have nothing to offer you. Although it is not our intention to attempt to sell you equipment, we must point out that learning and selling the techniques we are about to cover would enable you to pay for a circle/oval mat cutter in very short order. And, not to be ignored, it would also allow you to offer a complete range of matting services in your frameshop. There are a number of cutters available on the market, and we suggest that you compare several before making a decision on which one is best for you.

One of the keys to understanding the potential of a circle/oval cutter is to stop thinking of using it only on circular and oval artwork. There are many opportunities for using these shapes on other kinds of images, and we will be giving you some tips on how to recognize those that have potential for creativity. In the meantime, don't ignore the fact that a simple oval or circular mat can be quite attractive.

Basic Techniques For Using a Circle/Oval Mat Cutter

In many ways, a circle/oval mat cutter is easier to use than a straight line one. It may appear a bit intimidating, but with very little indoctrination and practice you should be able to execute precise, good looking mats. While there are several different brands available as we have mentioned, in our work we use the C & H Oval-Master®. And since that is the machine we are familiar with, we are going to use it as a reference for our tips and operating suggestions. While there may be some operating differences among the various brands, all the information we pass on should be applicable to other cutters as well.

CUTTING A BASIC CIRCULAR MAT

1. Cut your mat blank to the required size. (Let's use 16″ × 20″ for our example.) Place it in the cutter FACE UP. Circle and oval mats are cut in this manner, rather than face down as on the straight line cutter.

2. Set the horizontal guide on your cutter to 8″. (This is half the width of the mat blank.)

3. Set the vertical guide on your cutter to 10″. (This is half the length of the mat blank.)
    When the two guides are set in this manner, whatever you cut (circle or oval) will be centered in the mat blank. Just to reiterate: The HORIZONTAL guide is set for half the width of the mat, and the VERTICAL guide is set for half the length. (See photo of the cutter with guides on page 126.)

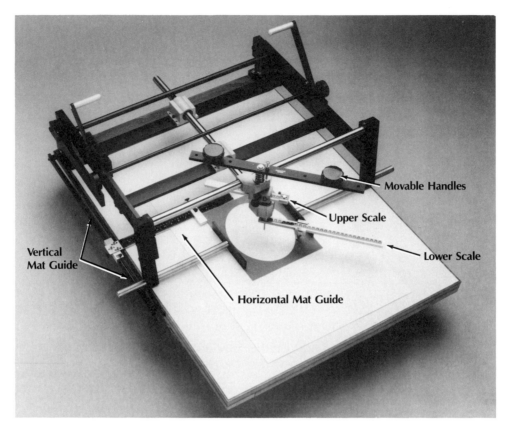

C & H/Bainbridge Model 789 Oval-Master®

In addition, on the Oval-Master cutter, there are two scales (an upper and a lower) that determine the size and the shape (circle or oval) of what you cut. (See photo of this assembly above.)

4. Set the upper scale to 0″. Set the lower scale on the diameter of the circle you want. Let's use 8″ for our sample. *Note: When cutting a circle mat, the top scale will always be set on 0″.*

5. Put the two-piece bevel blade in the holder, and lower the handle on the cutter into the cutting position. Remember that your mat should be FACE UP. Make certain that your mat hold-down arms are positioned so as not to interfere with the arc of the blade holder when cutting.

6. Turn the blade to the inside, so that when it begins to track it will mark on the dropout piece rather than on the visible border of your mat.

7. Put your right hand on the handle that is over the blade and begin to turn it clockwise, smoothly and not too fast. Once you get it turning,

gradually apply downward pressure to begin cutting. **Important:** *Don't jam the blade downward into the mat when you begin to cut.* This mechanism is spring loaded, so in order to achieve a good mat, you must apply the downward pressure gradually.

8. As soon as you have cut completely through the board, you should have an 8″ circle opening in the middle of a 16″ × 20″ board. It is that easy.

We would like to mention here that we usually put our circular openings in matboard with a square outer dimension, i.e., 20″ × 20″. This provides us with equal borders around the opening. To illustrate, we recommend that you size another blank to 16″ × 16″ and cut an 8″ circle into it. This will allow you to see what a circular opening with equal borders looks like and will also provide you with additional practice. If you should get confused, just refer to steps 1–8 above.

In the beginning, you will probably cut through into your underlayment piece farther than you need to. We find that most beginners complete the cut in the mat before they realize it. Don't be too concerned about it, as you will develop the right touch with just a little practice. We caution you about this since it's possible to go right through the underlayment and into the base of the cutter. This will ruin your blade and necessitate major resharpening.

BLADE CHOICES FOR THE CIRCLE/OVAL MAT CUTTER

There are three different blades that come with the Oval-Master: A one-piece straight cut blade, a one-piece bevel cut blade, and a two-piece bevel cut blade. All three can be sharpened and reused. For sharpening instructions, you should refer to the operator's manual. In addition, a couple of framing equipment suppliers now offer a compatible blade holder that takes a disposable Dexter® blade. This assembly is a substitute for the two-piece bevel blade only, but that is the one we use 90 percent of the time, and in our opinion a disposable blade will do a better job. (It is easy to replace and should always be sharp.) We recommend that you give both a try before making your choice.

Although we do use the two-piece bevel blade the majority of the time, there is one exception that you should be aware of: We do recommend that you use the *one-piece bevel blade* when cutting *small or narrow ovals*. (Anything under 6″ × 9″ would apply.) If you use a two-piece blade on an opening this small, the opening will appear to lean and visually it will not be perpendicular to the bottom of the mat. For all other mats, we recommend using the two-piece bevel blade, as it is closest to the bevel of the blade holder on the straight line cutter. This will make your life a lot simpler when we begin to execute combination cuts.

Now let's move along and execute the steps necessary to achieve a basic oval mat.

CUTTING AN OVAL MAT

1. Size a piece of matboard to 16″ × 20″.

2. Set the HORIZONTAL guide on the cutter to 8″ and the VERTICAL guide to 10″. This will insure that whatever you cut is in the center of your mat blank.

3. We are going to cut an 8″ × 10″ oval in our board, so set the BOTTOM scale on the cutter to 8″.

4. Set the TOP scale on the cutter to 2″ (the difference between 8″ and 10″).

5. Make sure your mat blank is FACE UP. Lower the handle to put the holder in cutting position and turn the blade to the inside of the mat before beginning. Just as you did with the circular mat, put your hand on the holder that is over the blade and begin to turn the arm smoothly. When you have it spinning, gradually apply pressure downward to begin cutting. Once you have started to apply the downward pressure, do not let up until you complete cutting through the board. You should now have an 8″ × 10″ oval opening in the center of a 16″ × 20″ board.

You will certainly want to put in some more practice time cutting both circles and ovals, but we are quite sure it will not be long before you are quite adept. The key points to remember are:

*   The mat blank should be in the cutter FACE UP.

*   Always turn your blade to the inside before you begin to cut.

- After you begin to turn the handle, gradually apply the downward pressure.

- Once you start to apply pressure downward, don't let up until you have cut completely through the matboard.

SUGGESTED PRICING: While some framers charge double their rectangular mat charge for a circular or oval opening, we do not feel that it is necessary. They are really quite easy to execute once you become familiar with the cutter and should require no additional labor. We would recommend that your charge be the same as for a rectangular single mat and be determined by the united inch charge for the kind of matboard that you are using.

Double Matting with Circles and Ovals

Circle and oval double mats are extremely easy to do as long as you are aware of one trick: ***The two mat blanks should be attached together before you begin cutting the outer mat***. We found that it is very difficult, if not impossible, to align the two mats perfectly if they are cut separately, so this technique is very important.

Let's run through one just to make sure you understand the procedure. We will create a 14″ × 14″ circular double mat with an 8″ opening in the outer mat and a ¼″ inner cuff.

1. Cut two pieces of matboard to size. Just as in rectangular double mats, the outer mat would be the size of your frame, and the inner mat should be approximately ½″ smaller on all four sides. Our sample mat is 14″ × 14″, so our inner mat blank should be approximately 13″ × 13″. It could be a little smaller than that, but we do not want to be too skimpy.

2. Using Scotch ATG tape, attach these two boards together. You should be sure to position the tape away from your opening and toward the outside border, so that you will not be cutting through it when you cut your openings.

3. We have already decided that our outer mat will have an 8″ circle opening, so 8″ is the setting of the blade holder on the lower gauge. As always when cutting a circle, the upper gauge should be set on 0″.

4. Set both of your guides on 7″. (Since this mat is square, one-half the width and one-half the length will be the same figure.)

DOUBLE OVAL OPENING MAT WITH ⅛″ INNER MAT

5. Put the two boards, which you attached together, into the cutter FACE UP and lower the handle placing the blade in cutting position. Turn the blade to the inside of the circle it is going to track.

6. Put your right hand on the handle, which is over the blade holder, and begin to rotate it smoothly. Apply downward pressure gradually, remembering not to jam the blade into the mat. Once you have begun to apply the pressure downward, don't let up until you have cut completely through the matboard. *Caution: Be careful not to cut all the way through both of the mats.* However, do not be concerned if you cut slightly into the under mat as it will not show. Once again, it is going to take a little practice to develop the right touch.

7. Once you complete cutting through the top mat, and *without lifting* the cutter handle, move your blade holder setting on the lower scale to 7½". (Since we want to have a ¼" cuff on this mat, we have to deduct that amount for each side of the circle: 2" × ¼" = ½".)

8. Turn your blade to the inside once again and cut out the circle in the bottom mat. You should now have completed a circular double mat with an inner mat that is exactly ¼" all the way around. If you had a problem with any part of this technique, or your mat did not come out as well as it should, we suggest that you start over and make another sample before you move on.

We emphasize again that you will never get quality results if you attempt to cut the two mats separately and then attach them together.

Now execute an oval double mat. The outside dimensions will be 11" × 14", with an 8" × 10" opening in the outer mat, and a ⅛" cuff on the inner mat. Your technique will be exactly the same as used on the preceding sample, so if you have any questions you should do a little reviewing. Use the two-piece bevel blade, but if the ovals appear to lean in the finished mat, switch to the one-piece bevel blade and try it again.

SUGGESTED PRICING: Since we feel it is not necessary to charge anything extra for circular and oval mats, the charge for this mat would be the same as for a rectangular double mat.

133

Using a "V-Groove" with Circle and Oval Mats

The easiest way to add a little something special to a circle or oval mat is our old friend the "V-Groove." Either the Regular or Slant Corner groove can be used quite effectively. We are going to have you make samples of both so that you can view the differences. Neither is better than the other, the choice is a design option for you and your customers. We have discovered through experience, though, that *"V-Grooves" used with circle and oval mats look better on the outside border rather than next to the opening.* You should keep this in mind when designing.

"V-GROOVE" WITH CIRCLE MATS

1. Cut two pieces of matboard to 14" × 14".

2. In the first cut a Regular "V-Groove" at 1". After completing the cutting and taping it back together, cut a 9" *circle* opening in the same board.

3. In the second board that you sized, cut a ⅜" Slant Corner "V-Groove" at 1¼". After completing the execution of that "V-Groove", cut a 9" *circle* opening in that board also.

Compare the two mats that you have completed and note the visual differences. Remember that neither one is better than the other, they both offer valid design.

Naturally, there are a number of possible options for placement of the "V-Groove" in your mat border as well as the amount of slant used in

14″ × 14″ Mat with
9″ Circle Opening,
"V-Groove" at 1″

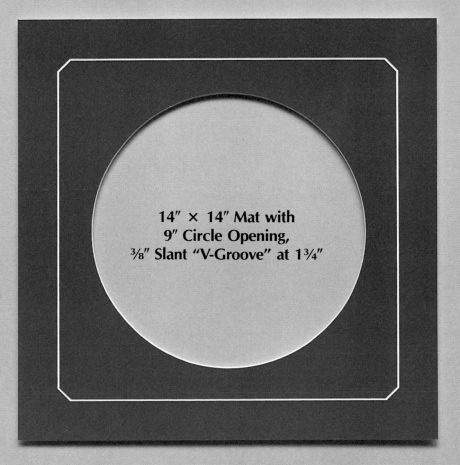

14″ × 14″ Mat with
9″ Circle Opening,
⅜″ Slant "V-Groove" at 1¾″

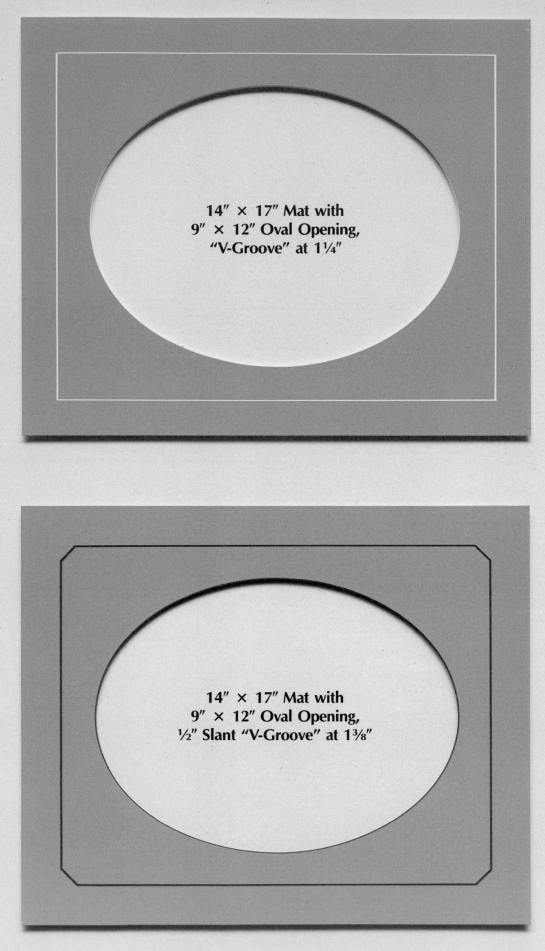

14″ × 17″ Mat with
9″ × 12″ Oval Opening,
"V-Groove" at 1¼″

14″ × 17″ Mat with
9″ × 12″ Oval Opening,
½″ Slant "V-Groove" at 1⅜″

the Slant Corner "V-Groove." This is where you should experiment and make a number of samples to have on hand. We have found it a very good idea not to assume that a design will not work until we have actually made a sample of it. Sometimes you stumble onto some surprising effects.

"V-GROOVE" WITH OVAL MATS

1. Cut two pieces of matboard to 14" × 17".

2. In the first, cut a Regular "V-Groove" at 1¼". Next, cut an *oval* opening 9" × 12" into the same board.

3. In the second board, cut a ½" Slant Corner "V-Groove" at 1⅜" and then follow with a 9" × 12" *oval* opening in the same mat. ***Note:*** *Always cut your "V-Groove" in a mat before you cut the opening.*

This will give you four samples to compare and should provide a feeling of how a "V-Groove" can enhance a circular or oval opening mat. It would also be a good idea to create some double mats with circular and oval openings and a "V-Groove." We're sure you can see that the possible combinations with these are almost endless, and while it is not practical to cut a sample of every one, you should have a few to work with.

> **SUGGESTED PRICING:** The regular united inch charge for the type of matboard that you use *plus* the united charge for your "V-Groove," be it Regular or Slant Corner. With double mats, you should charge for both boards *plus* the united inch charge for a "V-Groove" if used.

MORE DESIGN WITH "V-GROOVES" AND CIRCLE/OVAL OPENINGS

We want to point out that there is no reason you cannot use the more exotic "V-Grooves" that you have learned in conjunction with circle and oval openings. These would include:

16″ × 20″ MAT WITH 10″ × 14″ OVAL OPENING MAT WITH DOUBLE TRACK "V-GROOVE"

- Two regular "V-Grooves," ⅛" apart

- A regular "V-Groove" and a ¼" Slant "V-Groove," ¼" apart

- A Double Track "V-Groove" (see the photo)

The key to this of course is to make sure that you do not overdo when adding more design. Our objective as framers is never to compete with or overshadow the artwork and always to work within the limits of taste and restraint. It is extremely important to know when to quit. When in doubt, remember that *"less is more."*

SUGGESTED PRICING: The regular united inch charge for the type of board used *plus:*

- *For a pair of Regular "V-Grooves"*—.30/united inch (.15 per united inch per groove)

- For a pair of "V-Grooves"—one Regular and one Slant—.35/united inch

- For a Double Track "V-Groove"—.35/united inch.

Circular Corners

This will be our first corner to combine cutting on both the straight line cutter and the circle/oval machine. Our procedure for executing corners of this type is always the same; first cut on the circle/oval mat cutter and then move to the straight line cutter. With this in mind, let's get started.

1. Cut a piece of matboard to 16" × 20".

2. Determine the radius you would like to use for your round corner and set the LOWER scale on the circle/oval cutter to that figure. We are going to use 2" for this sample. *Remember, when executing a circle on this cutter, the upper scale must be set on 0".* The radius of the corner can be adjusted for any design result that you might wish to achieve. We recommend that you make up samples of many different versions once you become comfortable with the execution.

3. Set both of the mat guides on the circle/oval cutter by taking the width of border (we will use 3") and adding to it one-half of the circle diameter of 2" (3" + 1" would give us 4" for the two settings).

4. With both guides set on 4", cut a circle in all four corners of your 16" × 20" board. Be certain that you are using the two-piece bevel blade, as it is closest to the bevel of the straight line cutter which we will be using next.

5. Move to the straight line cutter and connect the four circles. This can be a little bit tricky and it is going to take some practice on your part. Because the bevels on the two cutters do not match perfectly, you will need to do some hand work to make them blend in just right.

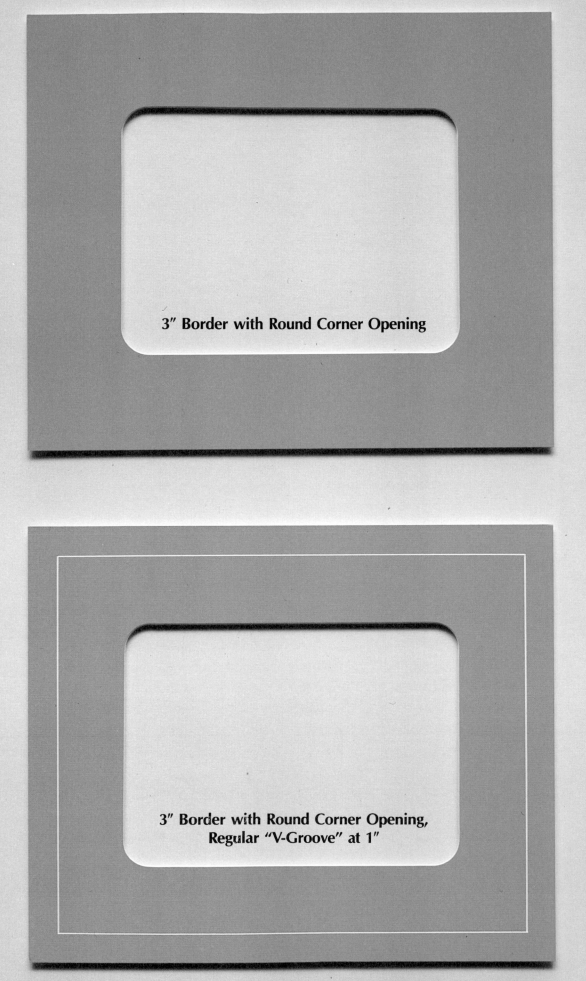

3" Border with Round Corner Opening

3" Border with Round Corner Opening,
Regular "V-Groove" at 1"

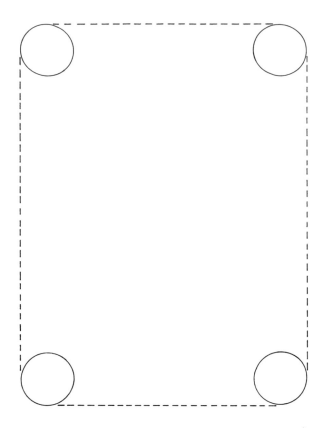

CONNECTING CIRCLES FOR ROUND CORNER MAT

We use 220 grit sandpaper and a very sharp razor blade. It *can* be done, so just keep trying until it becomes comfortable.

At this point, you should make additional samples of Circular Corners and include a "V-Groove" in them. The reasons are twofold and always the same. It will give you needed practice in executing the corner and provide the samples you will need for designing framing with your customers. We particularly like the way a Slant Corner "V-Groove" looks with a Round Corner mat. This is not to say that you should never use a Regular "V-Groove" with them, but the Slant Cornered one provides especially eye-catching design. (See the photo on page 143.)

SUGGESTED PRICING: Circular Corners are $20.00/mat. (Because of the additional time and hand work required to blend in the bevels on the combination cuts, a substantial charge is necessary to insure a profit.) The charges for the board and a "V-Groove" would be additional.

ROUND CORNER OPENING MAT

**3″ Border with Round Corner Opening
and ¼″ Slant Corner "V-Groove" at 2″**

The Kobe Corner

Before we give you the step-by-step instructions on how to create this corner, you might be interested in its background. Named after a town in Japan, the Japanese have been making frames with this type of corner for many years. We felt the shape would make an attractive mat corner, and after some experimentation were able to come up with a method for accomplishing it. Do not be misled into thinking that it works only on oriental subjects, for it is far more versatile than that. Use your imagination and creativity and get some up on display. This one will really wow your customers.

1. Begin by sizing a board to 16″ × 20″ or larger.

2. We are going to use a 2″ circle, so set the bottom scale on the oval cutter to 2″ and make certain that the top scale is on 0″.

3. Set *either* one of the mat guides on your oval cutter to the width of the border you would like to use *plus* one-half of your circle. (We will use 3″ for our border and one-half of the 2″ circle is 1″. So 3″ + 1″ = 4″.)

4. Set the *other* guide on the width of the border *plus* the diameter of the whole circle (3″ + 2″ = 5″).

5. With the two guides set as above, make a circle in each corner of your mat. Don't be concerned when the circles are not in the same place in all four corners.

6. Reverse the two mat guides. The one that had previously been set on 4″ should be moved to 5″ and the one that had been set on 5″ should now be on 4″.

KOBE CORNER MAT

**3″ Border with Kobe Corner Opening and
¼″ Slant Corner "V-Groove" at 2″**

7. With the guides reset, make another circle in each corner of the mat. These circles will intersect and create the points for your Kobe Corner.

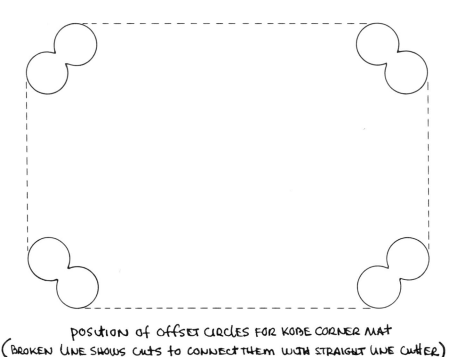

POSITION OF OFFSET CIRCLES FOR KOBE CORNER MAT
(BROKEN LINE SHOWS CUTS TO CONNECT THEM WITH STRAIGHT LINE CUTTER)

8. Move to the straight line cutter and connect up the circles you created in steps 3–7 above. This will complete your mat.

When connecting up the circles with your straight cutter, you face the same problems you did with Circular Corners. They are going to take some hand work and time to make them look perfect, but with a little practice you can do it. This Kobe Corner is really worth the effort, for when people visit your shop and see matting of this caliber, they are going to realize that you can accomplish work they have not seen in other frameshops.

Go ahead and cut two more Kobe Corners and put one of each type of "V-Groove" in your samples. We think you will find that they get easier and take less "doctoring" after you have completed a few.

> **SUGGESTED PRICING:** Kobe Corners are also $20.00/mat. We are sure you know by now that this is in addition to all other charges.

KOBE CORNER WITH A NOTCH

This is another of those corners that is accomplished by making a very slight modification of the basic cut, yet it has a distinctly different look.

1. Follow steps 1–8 for the basic Kobe Corner.

9. Set the mat guide on your straight line cutter to 3⅜". Mark your mat and cut out the notch in all four corners. (See shaded area in diagram.)

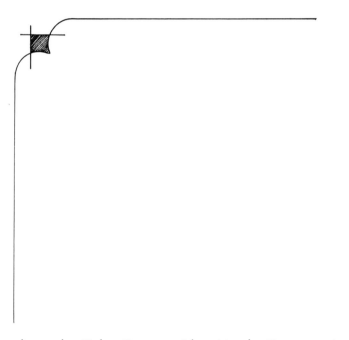

Now you have the Kobe Corner with a Notch. Compare it with the plain Kobe Corner which you cut previously and you will see that it does have a different, softer look. If you turn to page 164, you'll see a photograph of this corner used in a triple mat on a Pegge Hopper serigraph.

When you are making additional samples of this corner, experiment with notching them at settings other than 3⅜". A good place to try one would be 3½". We want to encourage you to experiment and look for new variations on your own.

SUGGESTED PRICING: Kobe Corners with a Notch are $20.00/mat.

3″ Border—Kobe Corner with a Notch Opening

3″ Border—Kobe Corner with a Notch Opening and ¼″ Slant Corner "V-Groove" at 1″

3″ Border—Kobe Corner with a Notch Opening and Two Regular "V-Grooves" a 2″ and 2¼″

Double Matting with Kobe Corners and Kobe with a Notch

You can get a fantastic double mat combination by putting together the corners we covered in the preceding two sections. These would be the Kobe Corner and Kobe Corner with a Notch.

Since you already know how to cut them both, all you need are the following tips.

- Before you begin, you will have to cut both of the matboards you are going to use to exactly the same size. This is another of the double mats that cannot be accomplished by gluing two boards together, so in order to get professional results *it is essential that the two blanks be identical*.

- Both combinations of the two corners are very effective in a double mat presentation:

    Kobe Corner on the outer mat and Kobe Corner with a Notch on the inner mat

    Kobe Corner with a Notch on the outer mat and Kobe Corner on the inner mat

- *Remember that your "V-Groove" should be cut in the outer mat before executing the corner.*

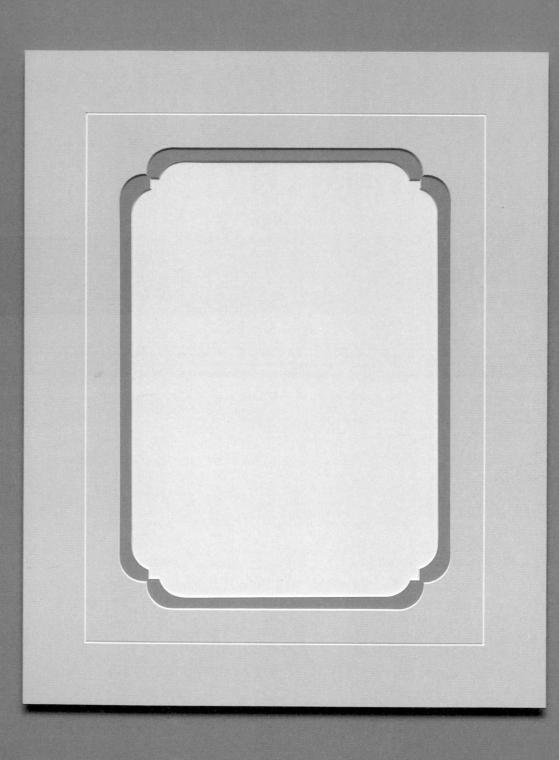

**3″ Border—Kobe Corner Opening Outer
Mat and Kobe Corner with a Notch
Opening Inner Mat**

3″ Border—Kobe Corner with a Notch
Opening Outer Mat and Kobe Corner
Opening Inner Mat

SUGGESTED PRICING: A double mat using either of the combinations on page 149 would be $40.00 ($20.00/mat). This would be in addition to your united inch charge for each of the boards *plus* a charge for the "V-Groove." Just to make absolutely certain that you are clear about how to price this one, let's figure a sample mat.

EXAMPLE: A 20" × 30" double Alphamat with a Slant Corner "V-Groove" and a Kobe Corner with a Notch outside mat and a Kobe Corner inside mat.

50 united inches × .80/united inch = **$40.00** (That is .30/united inch per mat *plus* .20/united inch for the Slant Corner "V-Groove.")
$20.00 for the Kobe Corner with a Notch mat
$20.00 for the Kobe Corner mat
A total charge of: $80.00

We know that you're thinking this is an outrageous price for a mat, but remember that you are selling design—not time and materials. If you use good taste and creativity with your designs, your customers will appreciate and be willing to pay for those skills. While you may not be able to charge exactly the same as we do, the point we want to reinforce is that you can expect some extra compensation. Stop thinking of yourself as just a picture framer but as a frame designer, and you are on your way.

Window Openings For Engraved Brass Plaques

Much of the artwork that your customers bring to you for framing is very personal to them. Anything that you can do with your framing design to make it even more so will meet with enthusiastic responses and guarantee repeat business. The technique we are about to teach you will certainly accomplish this. All you have to do to sell this one is to use it in some finished framing and display it prominently in your store.

These plaques were originally used on liners or frames for oil paintings and indicated the title, artist, and perhaps the artist's life years, if deceased. With just a little imagination, you can use it to indicate information that will make it very personal and special for your client.

Let's begin by cutting a piece of matboard to 20″ × 24″. This design won't look as well in smaller mats. You also need to know that we are going to use a 3″ border on the top and sides of our piece and a 3½″ border on the bottom. This is the first time we have required you to use offset borders, but it is necessary with this particular mat.

1. Set the circle gauge on your circle/oval cutter to 1½″. At the same time set the horizontal gauge on that cutter to 2″. (We are going to assume that this mat is for a horizontal image. Thus the 20″ dimension is the height and the 24″ dimension the width.)

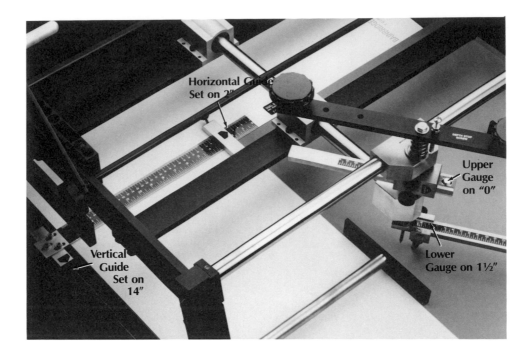

2. Set the vertical gauge on the cutter to one-half the width of the mat plus 2″ (one-half of 24″ = 12″ + 2″ = 14″).

3. Using the two-piece bevel blade, make a circle in the board.

4. Move *only* the vertical gauge, and set it on one-half the width of the mat − 2″ (one-half of 24″ = 12″ − 2″ = 10″) and at that setting make a second circle in the board.

5. Put the mat into your straight line cutter and using the mat guide, mark it at 2". Cut out this opening and "V-Groove" it. (You should be running your "V-Groove" into the middle of the circles you cut previously.)

"V-Groove" at 2" and Running into the Middle of the Two Circles

6. On the back of the mat, draw a line that bisects each of the circles and is perpendicular to the bottom border. (See Diagram A on page 156.) *If those lines are not perpendicular, the finished window will appear to lean.*

7. Measure ¼" from the top and the bottom of each circle and mark those points on the bisecting lines you drew in step 6. Draw lines connecting the points. (See Diagram B.)

8. Remove your mat guide from the straight line cutter and cut out the shape you have created. It is outlined in red in Diagram C.

9. Replace your mat guide onto the cutter, mark, and cut out the opening. Remember this mat has 3" on the sides and top and 3½" on the bottom. It should be easy for you to keep it straight since the plaque window is on the bottom.

10. Place a piece of matboard behind your window opening and mount the plaque on top of it with clear Silicone sealer. (Just a

LAYOUT FOR WINDOW OPENING FOR ENGRAVED PLAQUE

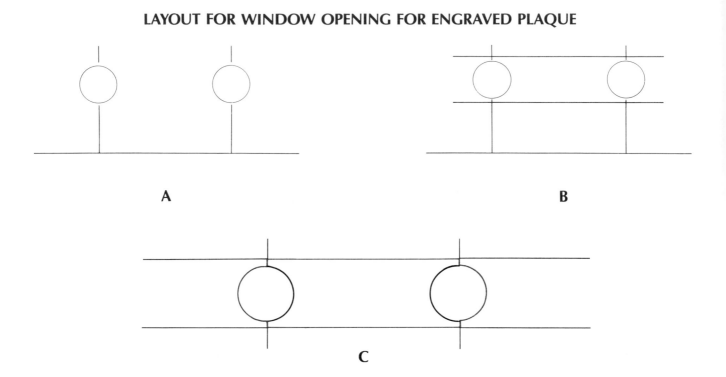

A

B

C

couple of small dabs is *plenty*.) Please also refer to the illustration on page 168 for an example of how great this mat design looks in a finished frame.

This is a great looking mat, and you should get good response when you display it.

The plaques are available from a number of different sources, and their advertisements appear regularly in *Decor* magazine. The one we have been using since I first began cutting this window is

BRASSCO ENGRAVING CO.
3631 Fairmont
P.O. Box 190107
Dallas, TX 75219

The people at Brassco are very nice and the service is excellent. They will send you sample plaques with different engraving styles and you'll be ready to go.

You should be aware that the plaques come in several different sizes. The instructions and settings that appear above are for the size A-45 plaque, which is the one we use about 90 percent of the time.

Occasionally (on mats with smallish outer dimensions) we do use the smaller A-35 plaque. Only one small adjustment is required to change the window size to fit. In step 2, change the setting of the vertical gauge to one-half the width of your mat plus 1¾" (instead of 2"). After cutting the first circle, move the gauge to one-half the width of the mat minus 1¾" and cut the second circle. That is all there is to it.

Once you have cut a few of these and are comfortable with the procedure, you can go ahead and add double and triple mats, too. There are numerous possibilities for you to explore with this new design.

SUGGESTED PRICING: The recommended charge for the plaque window is $25.00. This includes the cost of the plaque and having it engraved. (It will not cost you very much.) The $25.00 charge is in addition to the charge for the "V-Groove" and the type of matboard you use. Do not worry about price resistance on this design. It is such an elegant look that customers easily see the value. Remember, you are selling "creativity" and design, and that is very special.

5

CONCLUDING THOUGHTS

The possibilities for combining the designs and techniques we have discussed in this volume are almost endless. Naturally, some combinations will look better than others, but that judgment will depend a great deal on personal taste. The most important thought we can leave with you is that while experimentation is essential to your development as a "Creative" Mat Designer, you must always keep in mind the premise that *"less is more."* Use your good taste and restraint when designing with all your new "tricks" and don't be afraid to keep your mats understated and elegant.

If you're going to be using "Creative Matting," you must keep the frames themselves simple, clean, and uncluttered. It's very important that the mats and the mouldings not fight each other. Avoid using frames that are too wide and have the same visual weight as your mat. We lean toward "Caps" and profiles that have little or no ornamentation, and we also use a lot of aluminum. If you'll look through the illustrations of finished framing designs that follow, you will get an idea of the way we let our matwork be the "sizzle" in the framing presentation.

In closing, we sincerely hope you have enjoyed our ideas and will find them useful whether you are an experienced framer or just beginning a new career. GOOD LUCK, and our best wishes for lots of new business, "creative" satisfaction, and greater profits.

TITLE: Untitled **MEDIUM:** Handmade Paper **ARTIST:** Leanne Weissler
PUBLISHER: Trig Graphics, Dobbs Ferry, NY

TITLES: 1985 First of State New York Duck Stamp Print, 1986 New York Duck Stamp Print   ARTISTS: Larry Barton, David Maass   PUBLISHERS: Peterson Prints, Los Angeles, CA; National Wildlife Galleries, Fort Myers, FL

TITLE: Antique Map: Les Isles Antilles—1820   ARTIST: M. Bonne

TITLE: "Banana Leaf 3"   ARTIST: Pegge Hopper
PUBLISHER: Winn Publishing, Seattle, WA

TITLE: "Valerie—Age 4"
(Used by permission of Valerie McClure)

TITLE: Work 75-25 ARTIST: Haku-Maki

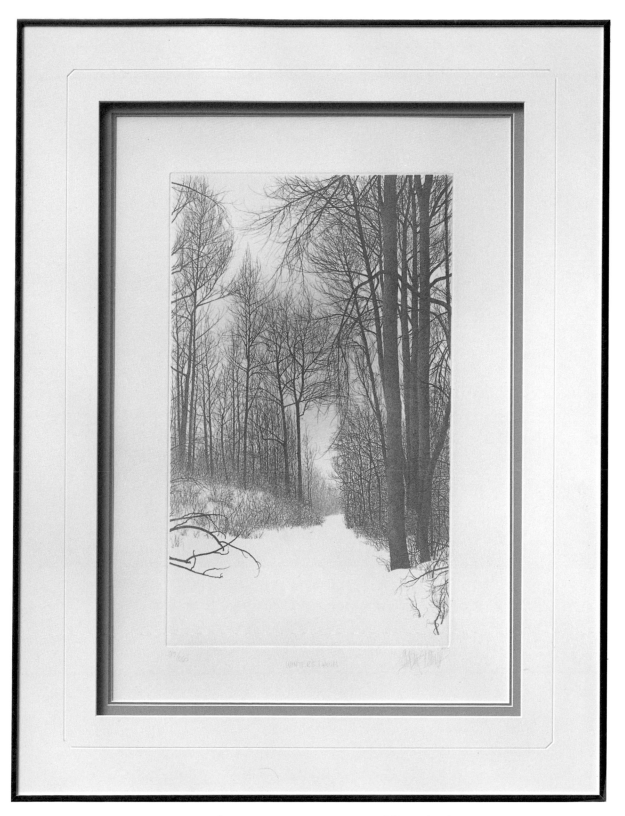

TITLE: "Winter's Dawn"   ARTIST: Franklin Galambos
PUBLISHER: J.L. Clark Fine Arts, Ltd., Cornwall, NY

TITLE: "Last Leaves"   ARTIST: Gunter H. Korus
PUBLISHER: Tilting at Windmills Editions, Manchester Center, VT

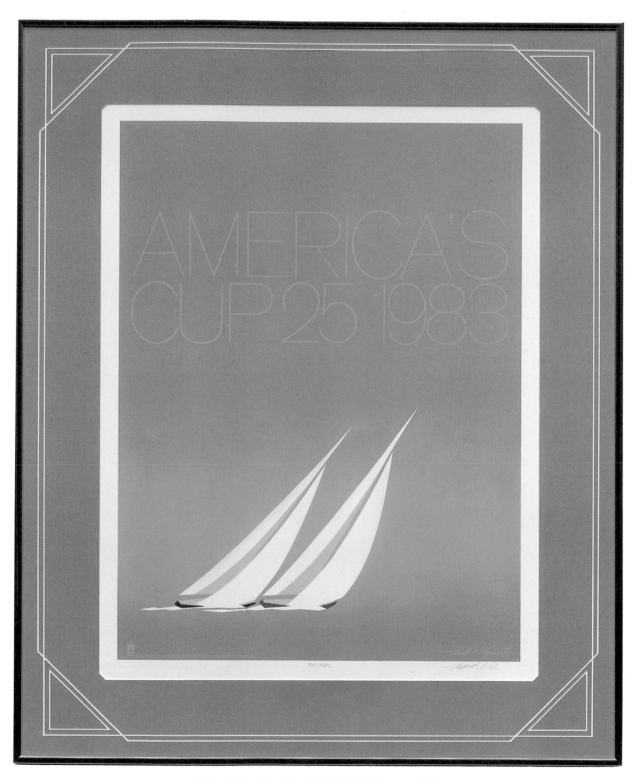

TITLE: "The Duel"   ARTIST: Keith Reynolds
PUBLISHER: Mystic Maritime Graphics, Mystic, CT

TITLE: "Edgewater" ARTIST: Virgil Thrasher
PUBLISHER: New York Graphic Society, Greenwich, CT

TITLE: "Gestalt"   ARTIST: Victor Vasarely
PUBLISHER: Editions du Griffon, Neuchatel/Suisse

**TITLES: "Friends," "Pet Pig," "Dark Goose"   ARTIST: Nancy Lubeck
PUBLISHER: The Artist, N. Pownal, VT**

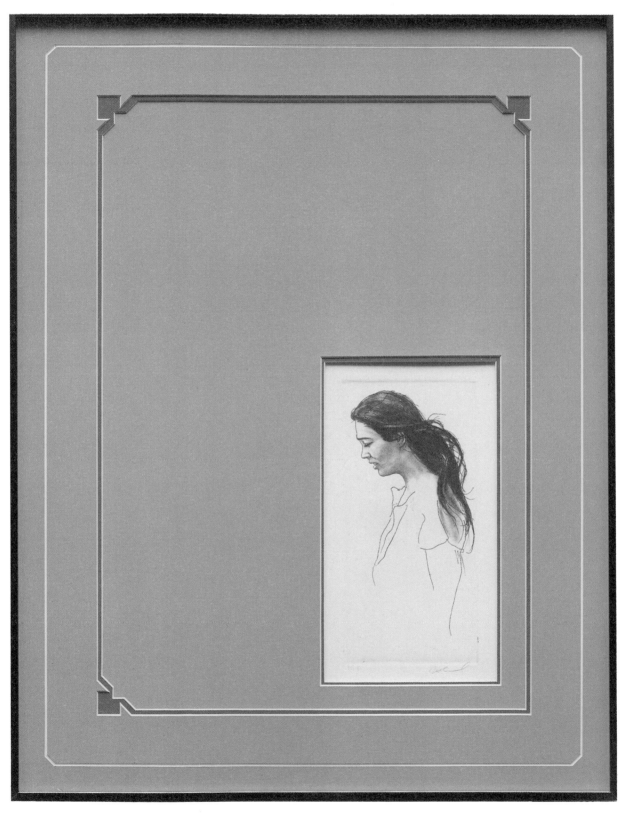

TITLE: "Girl's Head"   ARTIST: Harry McCormick
PUBLISHER: Bermond Art, Lake Success, NY

APPENDIX A
Pricing Summary

RECOMMENDED UNITED INCH PRICING

Regular or Paper matboard—.10 to .12 per united inch

Black Core matboard—.20 per united inch

Alphamat® or Alpharag® board—.30 per united inch

Fabric Matboards:
    Linen—.80 per united inch
    Suede—$1.00 per united inch
    Silk—$1.00 per united inch

"V-Grooves":
    Regular—.15 per united inch
    Slant Corner—.20 per united inch
    Pair of "Grooves" (two Regular)—.30 per united inch (.15/united inch/per groove)
    Pair of "V-Grooves" (one Regular and one Slant Corner)—.35 per united inch (.15/united inch + .20/united inch)
    Double Track "V-Groove"—.35 per united inch

Multiple matting—Rectangular, Circular, or Oval—should be the sum of the united inch charges for the types of board used:
    Double mat (Alphamat) = .60 united inch
    Triple mat (Alphamat) = .90 united inch

"V-Grooves" with Multiple Mats:
>   Double mat with "V-Groove" (Alphamat) = .75 united inch
>   (.60 + .15)
>   Triple mat with "V-Groove" (Alphamat) = 1.05 united inch
>   (.90 + .15)

Window Mounts:
>   Regular foam core—.20 united inch
>   Acid free foam core—.30 united inch

Inlay mats:
>   Single inlay (Alphamat)—.60 united inch (same as for a double mat)
>   Double inlay (Alphamat)—.90 united inch (same as for a triple mat)
>   Inlay mats with a "V-Groove"—same as above charges plus .15
>   united inch/per groove.

CHARGES FOR DECORATIVE CORNER DESIGNS

Offset Corners—$4.00/mat
Slant Corner Opening—$4.00/mat
Notch Cut Corner—$4.00/mat
The Deco Corner—$10.00/mat
The Baronial Corner—$10.00/mat
The Decoronial Corner—$10.00/mat
The Cutoff Decoronial Corner—$10.00/mat
The Keystone Corner—$20.00/mat
The "Cheater" Keystone Corner—$20.00/mat
Round Corners—$20.00/mat
The Kobe Corner—$20.00/mat
The Kobe Corner with a Notch—$20.00/mat
Window opening for an Engraved Plaque—$25.00 (This includes the cost
  of the plaque and engraving.)

APPENDIX B
Triple Mat Combinations

We don't need to tell you that there are an almost endless number of possible combinations for triple matting. After sixteen years of experimenting and designing framing for almost everything imaginable, we have discovered some favorite combinations that work in a wide variety of situations. We list them below in hopes that you too will find them useful. Naturally, they are only a tool to get your "creative" juices working, and you should spend time experimenting and finding standards of your own.

The numbers refer to Alphamat® colors, and each combination is listed with the outer mat border first and the two inner mats following. Please refer to our formulas on page 39 for recommended widths. The list is not in any particular order, but among the 21 combinations, you should be able to find at least one that will work on almost anything you come up against.

4-Ply White Rag, 8511, 8532
4-Ply White Rag, 8570, 8573
4-Ply White Rag, 8515, 8560
4-Ply White Rag, 8511, 8532
4-Ply White Rag, 8542, 8534
4-Ply White Rag, 8514, 8512
8521, 8503, 8508
8521, 4-Ply Ivory Rag, 8514
8503, 4-Ply Ivory Rag, 8508
8537, 8503, 8537
8525, 8539, 8531

8559, 8515, 8518
8559, 8515, 8552
8559, 8555, 8563
8520, 8525, 8538
8520, 8586, 8580
8520, 8532, 8531
8520, 8551, 8545
8520, 8504, 8572
8520, 8511, 8524
8520, 8521, 8512